Walk on Water

A 12-WEEK DEVOTIONAL ON TRUST, TURBULENCE, AND FIXING YOUR EYES ON JESUS

JULIE OSBORNE

Editor: Judy Keene
Editor & Consultant: Katrina Moody
Cover Design: Marilyn Eastes; Vizual Link LLC (vizuallink@gmail.com)
Author Photo: Stacy Able Photography

Published by Tales of Oz, LLC
Carmel, Indiana

Paperback ISBN: 979-8-9935521-0-1
Ebook - Kindle ISBN: 979-8-9935521-1-8
Hardback ISBN: 979-8-9935521-2-5

Dedication

To the One who seeks, encourages, rescues, and ultimately saves us. May this book draw us closer to you, Lord, and empower us to dip our toe in your Word so that, one day, we may dare to Walk on Water.

Table of Contents

Acknowledgments

First and foremost, I offer my deepest gratitude—and this book—back to the One who makes walking on water possible: My Lord and Savior, Jesus Christ. You inspired my writing through the Holy Spirit, gave me the necessary skills, and sent me the exact people and resources I needed in your perfect timing.

EARLY CAREER: CURRENT PUBLICATIONS

My career as a writer began when God led me to the office of *Current Publications* to apply for an unpaid internship position. Instead, I left that day as an editor! Thank you, Brian Kelly and Steve Greenberg, for believing in me despite my having zero experience, little training, and no clue what the responsibilities of a managing editor entailed when you offered me the job. My foundational years at *Current* truly launched my writing career.

EDITORS AND PUBLISHER

When I ventured out on my own as a freelance writer, I was blessed to cross paths with someone I desperately needed, even though I didn't know it at the time. God placed Judy Keene, who would become my editor, in the seat next to me at my first Bible study at Traders Point Christian Church. Judy, you have not only been an outstanding editor but an invaluable coach and teacher. This book would not have been possible without the years of writing tips, style guide pointers, and knowledge of the craft that you poured into me. Thank you!

God also brought another integral person to this project through my church, while serving on our online campus team during COVID. Each Sunday, I logged into Facebook at 11:00 AM to interact with our livestream guests and was particularly moved by one individual's prayers and heartfelt contributions in the chat. Katrina Moody inspired me so much that I *had* to meet her in person.

Since that time, we have become cherished sisters-in-Christ. Katrina is also my publisher. I smile when I think of how God sent me exactly who I needed to make this book a reality. Katrina, you are one of the most faith-filled, hardworking, talented, and loving people I have ever met, and I am honored and grateful to partner with you on this project. This book would not be possible without your endless God-given gifts—from formatting and editing to proofreading and everything in between. Thank you!

Design and Artwork

I must also recognize the beautiful cover and inside layout made possible by graphic designer extraordinaire, Marilyn Eastes. Your creative gifts are endless, and I'm honored to be a recipient, not only of your stunning work, but especially of your friendship. From the moment we met, in a small group at Traders Point Christian Church, I have been blessed by your joy-filled spirit, and now by your incredible talent. Thank you!

Community of Faith

Speaking of Traders Point Christian Church, I am eternally grateful to be a member of a family of faith where my pastors, Aaron Brockett and Ryan Bramlett, unapologetically preach the Gospel—even the difficult stuff—week in and week out. Your convicting messages have given me the courage to step out of my boat with this devotion and to speak boldly with my online Bible study teaching. Thank you!

WRITING TRIBES

I discovered another community along my writing journey when I surprised my beloved mom with tickets to the 2016 Erma Bombeck Writers' Workshop. This "Ermite" community has welcomed, supported, and encouraged Mom and me from the moment we arrived. I am especially thankful for Erma workshop leader, coach, and friend Susan Pohlman for empowering me to find my writer's voice. We need a reunion in Santa Fe!

In an effort to increase my platform and soften my disdain for social media promotion, I joined YPM, Your Platform Matters, and have been blessed by the encouraging members and passionate leader, Ann Kroeker. This community has helped my attitude and interaction with social media become more positive, and Ann's extensive knowledge has provided many useful golden nuggets. While I yearn to spend my days writing, I know being an active social media participant is critical to success. I will keep trying, thanks to YPM.

FRIENDS AND FAMILY

There are so many individuals I could add to this list, but a few I must mention:

Kandice Richey, you have been by my side through the valleys and mountaintops, and I can't imagine this life without you. You always show up and make time to encourage and love me as a true sister. Thank you for your selfless devotion, unwavering support, and never-ending patience. You are my angel on earth.

Mark Sigman, you have been a true brother since God placed me in the house next door. Your soup that shows up at my door when I'm sick, early morning shuttles to the airport, and willingness to help out whenever needed have been a constant reminder of God's love. And, you actually unknowingly planted the seeds for this book. Brother, you're stuck with me!

Dr. Joan Malick, you have been my cheerleader and living Barnabas since we met over two decades ago. I am forever grateful for your wisdom, chats over lattes, and the endless prayers and encouraging letters that show up in my mailbox. Jesus in the flesh has shown up through you.

I also want to recognize the dedicated members of my Sunday night Bible study group for their overwhelming support and willingness to read this devotional and provide valuable feedback before publishing. I cherish our time together and know God is at work. I've led groups for 25+ years, but this one is truly special.

Of course, I want to thank the joys of my life—my children, Nate and Carolyn. There has been no greater gift in my life than both of you. May you always remember one of my most important life lessons, "Live to Make God Smile." Although I'm a writer now, my favorite and best job title will always be "Mom."

And, last but certainly not least, none of this would be possible without my beloved mom, Lori Mansell. Throughout my life, you have encouraged, loved, and supported me. You are "Pixie Dust," and I have been a grateful recipient of the joy you sprinkle wherever you go. Your sacrifices through the years made my education and career possible, and now we're both writers. May we continue to travel this journey together. And, YES, Toto's book is coming soon. I love you, Mama!

Introduction

He walked on water.

Not just Jesus.

There was another person in the story who experienced this miracle moment.

"Then Peter got down out of the boat, walked on the water and came toward Jesus." (Matthew 14:29)

Peter, a mere fisherman, made a beeline toward the Lord *on the water*. Seriously, how is that even possible?

Like Peter, we believe in a God of impossibilities, but we have an important role to play.

For Peter, it began with *trust*. The next step was *action*. He left the comfort zone of the boat, stepping out of his secure environment and into the deep water, not knowing what would happen next.

It was a defining moment—a huge leap of faith with no one to keep him afloat but Jesus.

And it worked! Peter took one step, then another, drawing closer to the Lord. His faith and trust in Jesus resulted in his own miracle.

At least for a moment...

As Peter walked on the turbulent water, something shifted. The storms swirling around him hijacked his focus, and fear immediately overcame him. When Peter's gaze moved from Jesus to the terrifying waves, doubt took over and he went down—FAST. As Peter plunged into the dark abyss, he desperately needed a rescue, and Jesus, of course, was right there. He had not moved.

Jesus invites us to walk with him and to trust him, especially through the inevitable storms of life. We, like Peter, can experience the miraculous power of walking on water—but only if we keep our eyes fixed on Jesus and take that first step of faith.

Walk on Water is a 12-week devotional designed to help you do just that. Based on Matthew 14:22-33 and featuring 40+ compelling biblical stories, this book is a microcosm of the Christian walk: bold steps of faith, paralyzing fear, worldly distractions, and the desperate call out for Jesus' rescue.

Through these pages, you will read stories of real people who struggled, failed, and longed for their own "walk on water" moment. Some succeeded; others did not. But God honored their attempts and desire to be faithful, just as he honors yours.

All it takes is a few minutes each day to read the devotion and prayer, allowing the Holy Spirit to speak to you. There is also a dedicated space for reflection on the week's messages: to pray, journal your thoughts, and take another "STEP" closer to our Lord.

Finally, just as Jesus invited Peter out of the boat, this book provides an opportunity for you to "Invite a Friend." In the back section, you'll find additional questions designed to share and discuss over the phone or a cup of coffee.

Jesus is waiting for you to step out of your comfort zone and embark on this adventure with him. Let's walk on water toward Jesus, together!

Send

Immediately Jesus made the disciples get into the boat and go on ahead of him to the other side, while he dismissed the crowd.

— MATTHEW 14:22

Week 1 – Day One

Immediately Jesus made the disciples get into the boat and go on ahead of him to the other side, while he dismissed the crowd.

— MATTHEW 14:22

A miracle had just occurred. With a hungry crowd before him, Jesus had turned five loaves of bread and two fish into a huge feast, feeding 5,000 followers. Instead of giving the disciples a break, he "immediately" sent them away—onward to their next destination. Jesus had a plan and a purpose, and there was no time for rest. Next, Jesus dismissed the crowd. The day's work was now complete.

Just like the disciples, Jesus sends us out into the world. In fact, his final words before ascending into heaven were what we know as the Great Commission: "Therefore go and make disciples of all nations, baptizing them in the name of the Father and of the Son and of the Holy Spirit, and teaching them to obey everything I have commanded you. And surely I am with you always, to the very end of the age." (Matthew 28:19-20)

Sometimes we question his timing, his placement, and the difficulties that often arise. But his plan is perfect, even if we are sent directly into a storm as we will soon discover with this story.

Despite our struggles, Jesus never leaves us alone. He met his disciples right where they were, removing obstacles along the way. Now, he is eager to meet you right where you are through these pages.

Whether you're new to the Bible or a lifelong student, there's always a fresh message and lesson waiting for you. All you need to do is show up for five minutes each day with an eagerness to grow closer to the Lord.

QUESTION

God would like to send you on this journey to step into his Word daily. Are you ready? If not, what is your obstacle?

PRAYER

Lord, you send us out with a calling and purpose—and sometimes even directly into a storm. Please strengthen our faith through this study, and remind us that we are never alone. You are with us every step of the way. Amen.

DIG DEEPER

The Great Commission — Matthew 28: 16-20

Week 1 – Day Two

"I am sending you out like sheep among wolves. Therefore be as shrewd as snakes and as innocent as doves. Be on your guard; you will be handed over to the local councils and be flogged in the synagogues."

— MATTHEW 10:16–17

How would you like that for a pep talk before leaving on a very important mission! Jesus certainly didn't mince words or shy away from telling his disciples that their work ahead would not be easy. On top of that, they were not to take anything with them except the clothes on their back and the sandals on their feet. There would be no compensation, hotel reservations, or even meals provided. And they would likely be rejected by many—beaten and possibly even arrested. Jesus was sending them out not only into unknown territory but into enemy land.

As disciples, Jesus will inevitably send us into places or situations where we don't want to go. The biblical narrative is not our cultural norm, and our message will certainly stand out and often be met with resistance, cynicism, and sometimes attacks. It will not be easy. While we likely won't be flogged or beaten, there are still martyrs today in certain parts of the world who are risking their lives by sharing the gospel message.

But, just like the first disciples, we have nothing to fear with the guidance of God's Word and the Holy Spirit: "But when they arrest you, do not worry about what to say or how to say it. At that time you will be given what to say, for it will not be you speaking, but the Spirit of your Father speaking through you." (Matthew 10:19–20)

QUESTION

What are you risking to share the message of Jesus? Will you do it anyway?

PRAYER

Lord, you send us out into a world that is not following you. Sometimes we are afraid of the unknown or the resistance we will face. Please strengthen and guide our steps so that we can be faithful in spreading your Word and message. Amen.

DIG DEEPER

Jesus Sends out Twelve — Matthew 10:1–42, Luke 9:1–11, Mark 6:7–13

Week 1 – Day Three

Moses said to the Lord, "Pardon your servant, Lord. I have never been eloquent, neither in the past nor since you have spoken to your servant. I am slow of speech and tongue." The Lord said to him, "Who gave human beings their mouths? Who makes them deaf or mute? Who gives them sight or makes them blind? Is it not I, the Lord? Now go; I will help you speak and will teach you what to say." But Moses said, "Pardon your servant, Lord. Please send someone else."

— *EXODUS 4:10–13*

Moses didn't want to go. Can you blame him? God was sending him back to Egypt to ask Pharaoh, Egypt's king, to release the Israelites. This was a big ask as they were Pharaoh's main resource used as slave labor to build Egypt's epic pyramids. Pharaoh was not going to back down easily and release over 600,000 men! (Exodus 12:37–38)

Like Moses, we, too, may be reluctant when God calls us into difficult situations. We can make excuses—we don't have the talents, time, or treasures. But God knows exactly what we need to accomplish his purposes and, in Moses' case, who he needed. Moses had a brother, Aaron, who was an eloquent speaker and could deliver a message with power and persuasion. God also equipped Moses with a staff that performed signs and wonders to showcase his divine power for all of Egypt to see.

God provided Moses with exactly what and who he needed to convince Pharaoh to free the Israelites, and he sends us exactly what we need, too. There is no need to fear.

QUESTION

Have you ever felt ill-equipped for something God was calling you to do? What was the result?

PRAYER

Lord, just like Moses, you send us into difficult situations that can seem impossible at times, but we know we are never alone. You go with us and also send us what we need to accomplish your mission. Help us to never let fear get in our way. Amen.

DIG DEEPER

Israelites Oppression and Escape — Exodus 1–15

Week 1 – Day Four

Now an angel of the Lord said to Philip, "Go south to the road —the desert road—that goes down from Jerusalem to Gaza." So he started out, and on his way he met an Ethiopian eunuch, an important official in charge of all the treasury of the Kandake (which means "queen of the Ethiopians").

— ACTS 8:26–27A

It was a divine meeting in the middle of the desert. Philip had no idea why God was sending him there, but he went without pause. He left without even a question. God was planning an unlikely meeting in a strange place—but with an eternal purpose. Philip would be the one who would share the gospel message with a traveling foreigner, who would then take Jesus' message back to a continent.

I don't know about you, but if an angel appeared and asked me to head to the desert with no explanation, I would have some questions. What on earth will I be doing there? How long will I be gone? The desert? Why? But not Philip. He immediately took off on his journey and soon crossed paths with an important Ethiopian official who was thirsty to learn more about the Scriptures. Because of his obedience, Philip was able to explain the good news about Jesus to the eunuch and, as a result, this stranger in the desert was baptized.

Sometimes we don't know why God is sending us into a specific situation or difficult circumstance, but we know he sends us for a reason and with an eternal purpose. We just need to trust and obey even when we don't understand.

QUESTION

Has God ever given you a clear command to "Go" that made you uncomfortable? How did you react? What was the result?

PRAYER

Lord, sometimes you command us to "Go" somewhere we don't understand or into situations that make us uncomfortable. Philip reminds us that you send us with a plan and a purpose. Help us to trust you, especially in those uncertain times. Amen.

DIG DEEPER

Philip and the Ethiopian Eunuch — Acts 8:26–40

Week 1 – Day Five

The Lord had said to Abram, "Go from your country, your people and your father's household to the land I will show you. I will make you into a great nation, and I will bless you; I will make your name great, and you will be a blessing. I will bless those who bless you, and whoever curses you I will curse; and all peoples on earth will be blessed through you."

— GENESIS 12:1–3

Leave your life as you know it behind. That is basically what God instructed Abraham to do. It was an epic move to a foreign territory over 600 miles away that was currently being occupied by other nations—and they were not friendly ones! The current landowners weren't going to give up their homeland without a fight. What God was asking Abraham to do would not have made sense at the time, but God had a much bigger plan and purpose in mind.

With God's words alone, Abraham headed out into the unknown with only a promise to hang onto, without a question or hesitation:

"So Abram went, as the Lord had told him; and Lot went with him. Abram was seventy-five years old when he set out from Harran. He took his wife Sarai, his nephew Lot, all the possessions they had accumulated and the people they had acquired in Harran, and they set out for the land of Canaan, and they arrived there." (Gen. 12:4–5)

God's promise to Abraham would not be fulfilled in his lifetime, but he played an integral role in moving it forward. Because Abraham obeyed God's commission, his descendants—over 400 years later—would indeed conquer the Promised Land.

QUESTION

God sends us out not only with a plan and a purpose, but also with a promise. Is there a promise that you hang onto through uncertain times?

PRAYER

Lord, we are grateful for your promises. Sometimes that's all we have to cling to when we struggle to understand. Please help us to trust you, especially in those difficult moments. Amen.

DIG DEEPER

God's Call & Promise to Abraham — Genesis 12:1–9

Take a Step

Jesus sends us out into his world to accomplish his purposes—"Go make disciples." As we learned this week, he sent the disciples out to spread his message, knowing they would face resistance. He sent reluctant Moses to Pharaoh with a seemingly impossible request. He sent Philip to the desert without an explanation and Abraham to a new land with only a promise.

Now Jesus is sending you. Will you go?

STEP—WHAT SMALL STEP CAN YOU TAKE TODAY?

TRUST—WILL YOU TRUST AND SURRENDER TO THE LORD?

ENCOURAGE—WHO CAN ENCOURAGE YOU ALONG YOUR JOURNEY?

PRAY—PRAY FOR THE LORD TO GIVE YOU STRENGTH AND DIRECT YOUR NEXT STEPS.

Pray

After he had dismissed them, he went up on a mountainside by himself to pray.

— MATTHEW 14:23A

Week 2 – Day One

After he had dismissed them, he went up on a mountainside by himself to pray.

— MATTHEW 14:23A

It was a long night. Alone up on the mountain as he prayed, Jesus must have been bone-weary after feeding over 5,000 followers. Just gathering leftovers and cleaning up after the masses would have led to complete exhaustion. So he took a break to refuel and find refreshment with his Father. We don't know what happened in their time together, but we know it was fused with power. Another miracle was on the horizon.

There are many stories in the Bible in which Jesus took time alone to be with God. Just like in this story after a great success in preaching and feeding 5,000 people, he went off to pray. Sometimes he prayed alone, but he also prayed with his disciples—as well as in front of crowds like at his baptism. He prayed for guidance before choosing

12 disciples and all along his journey when things were going well and his ministry was spreading.

He also prayed in times of sorrow, including right after his cousin John the Baptist was beheaded. He prayed in a garden when he knew his death was imminent and even on the cross for those who tortured him, "Father, forgive them, for they do not know what they are doing." (Luke 23:34) No matter the circumstance, Jesus prayed.

Whether we are in a season of abundance or sorrow, we must take the time to commune with our heavenly Father. Jesus took prayer seriously, and if we are to be true Christ followers, so should we.

QUESTION

Is prayer a regular part of your life? How can you make space in your busy days to commune with the Lord?

PRAYER

Lord, thank you for the opportunity to talk with you anywhere and at any time. Please help us to make time with you a priority and to listen for your guidance, just as Jesus did. Amen.

DIG DEEPER

Jesus Prayed — Luke 3:21, Luke 6:12, Luke 5:16, Luke 9:28, Luke 22:40–44, Matthew 27:46, Luke 23:46, Mark 14:32

Week 2 – Day Two

This, then, is how you should pray: "Our Father in heaven, hallowed be your name,"

— MATTHEW 6:9

"Our Father in heaven, hallowed be your name, your kingdom come, your will be done, on earth as it is in heaven. Give us today our daily bread. And forgive us our debts, as we also have forgiven our debtors. And lead us not into temptation, but deliver us from the evil one." (Matthew 6:9–13)

The Lord's Prayer. Most of us have heard it, many repeat it weekly in church. But have you ever stopped to understand its meaning—and follow it? Let's read it slowly now.

The prayer starts with recognizing the awesomeness of God and the realization that his kingdom will reign on earth one day. There is a posture of humility with the words, *"your will* be done." It's not about us getting what we desire, but surrendering to the Lord's will.

Next is a request for what we need—our daily bread—not necessarily what we want. God's daily provision for the Israelites in the desert (Exodus 16) assures us that he will provide exactly what we need in his perfect timing.

Then there's that word—forgive. Jesus knows we live in a fallen world. We need his forgiveness, but we also need to forgive others.

Lastly, this prayer warns us not to fall into temptation as Adam and Eve did in the Garden of Eden. (Genesis 3) Jesus' final words of the Lord's Prayer serve as a sober reminder that we need God's protection every single day. Satan, the evil one, is at work in our world as he "prowls around like a roaring lion looking for someone to devour." (1 Peter 5:8)

QUESTION

When you recite the Lord's Prayer, what is the most challenging part to put into practice?

PRAYER

Lord, we thank you for teaching your disciples, and now us, how to pray. Let us approach you with a posture of humility so that we may surrender to your will. Amen.

DIG DEEPER

Jesus' Teachings on Prayer — Matthew 6:5–15, Luke 11:1–13, Mark 11:24–26

Week 2 – Day Three

In her deep anguish Hannah prayed to the Lord, weeping bitterly. And she made a vow, saying, "Lord Almighty, if you will only look on your servant's misery and remember me, and not forget your servant but give her a son, then I will give him to the Lord for all the days of his life, and no razor will ever be used on his head."

— 1SAMUEL 1:10–11

She cried out to the Lord. Hannah had not been able to conceive a child, and she felt hopeless. So, she dropped to her knees and did the only thing she could do—she prayed. Not only did she ask for a son, but she seemingly made a deal with God. If she birthed a son, she would give her child right back to the Lord "for all the days of his life." She wanted a baby so badly that she was willing to do the unimaginable—give him up.

God heard Hannah's prayers and delivered a son, Samuel. (In Hebrew, Samuel means "heard by God.") As difficult as it must have been, Hannah followed through with her vow. After weaning Samuel, she brought him to the temple and dedicated his life to the Lord. She left her beloved toddler there with a priest she had only briefly met a year earlier. I don't know if I could have done that willingly, but Hannah did. Not only that, she then worshipped God with a prayer of gratitude. Because of her trust in the Lord and sacrifice of her son, under the guidance of Eli the priest, Samuel grew up to become a great prophet, anointing David as king.

Just like Hannah, God hears and answers prayers—just not always in our way or timing. And as we pray, even though the circumstance may not change, God is at work changing and growing us.

QUESTION

When have you cried out to God for something that you desperately wanted? What was the result?

PRAYER

Lord, we know you hear our prayers and answer them. Please give us strength to keep on praying and waiting on you. We trust in your timing and perfect plan. Amen.

DIG DEEPER

Hannah's Story — 1 Samuel 1
Hannah's Prayer — 1 Samuel 2:1–10

Week 2 — Day Four

"So give your servant a discerning heart to govern your people and to distinguish between right and wrong. For who is able to govern this great people of yours?"

— 1 KINGS 3:9

He could have asked God for anything: wealth and prosperity; power to conquer kingdoms; enemies to be defeated; beautiful wives; monuments in his honor. But he didn't request any of that. Instead, Solomon appealed for wisdom.

Scripture doesn't tell us how old Solomon was when he took the throne after his beloved father King David died, but he clearly did not see himself ready for the job. While many new kings may have tried to "Fake it till you make it," Solomon had humility in sharing his weakness and insecurity with God. And, he was rewarded for it.

Not only did God grant Solomon what he requested, but far more: "I will do what you have asked. I will give you a wise and discerning heart, so that there will never have been anyone like you, nor will there ever be. Moreover, I will give you what you have not asked for —both wealth and honor—so that in your lifetime you will have no equal among kings." (1 Kings 3:12–13)

Because of God's favor, Solomon did indeed become a great king. Unfortunately, near the end of his life, Solomon made mistakes (big ones!) that had generational consequences. "As Solomon grew old, his wives turned his heart after other gods, and his heart was not fully devoted to the Lord his God, as the heart of David his father had been." (1 Kings 11:4)

Despite his failures, Solomon is still known as one of the wisest and greatest kings of Israel, securing peace, prosperity, and a united kingdom during his 40-year reign.

Question

If you could ask God for anything, what would it be? (You can!)

Prayer

Lord, we need you. We, like Solomon, struggle with discerning between good and evil. Please give us the wisdom and humility of Solomon so that we may walk in your will and surrender to your ways. Amen.

Dig Deeper

Solomon's Rule — 1 Kings 1–11

Week 2 – Day Five

He withdrew about a stone's throw beyond them, knelt down and prayed, "Father, if you are willing, take this cup from me; yet not my will, but yours be done." An angel from heaven appeared to him and strengthened him. And being in anguish, he prayed more earnestly, and his sweat was like drops of blood falling to the ground.

— LUKE 22:41–44

Jesus, the perfect, sinless man who was both fully God and fully human dropped to his knees in desperation with a life-changing prayer that had eternal consequences. In the Garden of Gethsemane, with blood pooling around him, Jesus cried out to his Father to remove the great suffering he would soon face. We all know what happened next.

God said "No." He denied his one and only Son deliverance from a horrifying death by crucifixion. God could have intervened and granted Jesus' request—but he didn't. And, sometimes he doesn't grant ours either. This truth can be difficult to understand and even more heart wrenching to accept. In our seasons of suffering, we want God to move, and we may pray fervently—for years—for a situation to change. But despite our steadfast prayers, suffering remains.

On that dark day we know as Good Friday, God had a clear view of his own tortured Son hanging lifelessly on a bloody cross, but he knew it was for a greater purpose—for us! Jesus' unimaginable suffering was necessary for our salvation to be secured and for our sins to be forgiven. It was God's plan all along.

Sometimes God says "No" to our prayers and allows our current circumstances to remain—just like he did for his beloved Son.

QUESTION

How do you respond to unanswered prayers? Have you seen God's hand at work even when the situation didn't change?

PRAYER

Lord, we trust you and know that your plans are better than our own. Comfort us in our anguish when our prayers don't align with your will, and make your presence known to us in our times of suffering. Amen.

DIG DEEPER

Jesus Prays in the Garden of Gethsemane — Luke 22:39–46, Matthew 26:36–46, Mark 14:32–42

Take a Step

Jesus prayed—a lot! He taught his disciples (and us) how to pray and gave us many examples in his Word. We learned that God doesn't always answer prayers in our desired way or timing—and sometimes he says "No," as he did to Jesus in his most desperate moment. But there are also examples where God granted the requests of his people. Hannah prayed for a son, and God delivered, and Solomon prayed for wisdom and became one of the greatest kings of all time.

NOW IT'S YOUR TURN. ARE YOU READY TO MAKE PRAYER A PRIORITY IN YOUR DAILY LIFE?

STEP—WHAT SMALL STEP CAN YOU TAKE TODAY?

TRUST—WILL YOU TRUST AND SURRENDER TO THE LORD?

ENCOURAGE—WHO CAN ENCOURAGE YOU ALONG YOUR JOURNEY?

PRAY—PRAY FOR THE LORD TO GIVE YOU STRENGTH AND DIRECT YOUR NEXT STEPS.

Storms

Later that night, he was there alone, and the boat was already a considerable distance from land, buffeted by the waves because the wind was against it.

— MATTHEW 14:23B–24

Week 3 – Day One

Later that night, he was there alone, and the boat was already a considerable distance from land, buffeted by the waves because the wind was against it.

— MATTHEW 14:23B–24

Jesus sent his disciples directly into a storm. Seriously? They were likely exhausted after serving over 5,000 people, but instead of rest they ended up in a rocking boat. With waves rising around them and lightning striking above, they clung to the rails for their lives.

This doesn't make sense. It almost seems like punishment to the group of people who were working side by side with Jesus to spread his message. They were the chosen ones who were closest to Jesus, so how could this happen? Why wouldn't the author of creation send a sunny day with calm waters so they could rest, regain their strength, and recharge?

We don't know the answer, but we do know that Jesus always has a plan and a purpose, and this time it was much bigger than the threatening waves surrounding them. Jesus knew the storms would come to an end, and his disciples would be strengthened through them.

Whether they are swirling around us or within us, storms are something we try to avoid. But as this story unfolds, we will learn that Jesus often uses storms to grow, correct, and strengthen his people. In John 16:33, Jesus reminds us, "In this world you will have trouble. But take heart! I have overcome the world."

Storms are inevitable, but the creator of the storms has a purpose in them.

QUESTION

What struggle(s) are you currently facing that God may be using to grow your faith?

PRAYER

Lord, we don't like storms in our work, relationships, homes—any part of our lives. Please make your presence known when difficulties arise so that our faith may be strengthened. Amen.

Week 3 – Day Two

A furious squall came up, and the waves broke over the boat, so that it was nearly swamped. Jesus was in the stern, sleeping on a cushion. The disciples woke him and said to him, "Teacher, don't you care if we drown?"

— MARK 4:37–38

Jesus was sleeping. With hurricane-force winds battering the boat he remained in a deep slumber. Jesus may have been unmoved, but the disciples were not. You can only imagine their panic when the water began to breach the sides of the boat and fill it. They were going down with the ship while their leader was counting sheep!

When they awoke Jesus, his first words were of rebuke to the wind and waves, "Quiet! Be still!" Immediately the storm subsided, and the waters became calm. You could probably hear a pin drop (or plink) in the bottom of that boat, with looks of wonder on the disciples' faces.

Jesus was not done with his admonition and next turned to his disciples, "Why are you so afraid? Do you still have no faith?" (Mark 4:40) Despite being in Jesus' presence and experiencing many miraculous healings, those closest to him *still* could not grasp his true divine identity. "They were terrified and asked each other, 'Who is this? Even the wind and the waves obey him!'" (Mark 4:41)

On that stormy day, Jesus showcased his power by immediately halting a dangerous squall. If Jesus can calm the winds on demand, certainly he can change the course of any storm we encounter.

QUESTION

When trials and tribulations arrive in your life, do you trust the Lord? Even when he doesn't calm the storm?

PRAYER

Lord, help us to remember who you are, especially when difficult times arise in our lives. Calm our fears and remind us of your great power, love, and mercy. Amen.

DIG DEEPER

Jesus Calmed the Storm — Mark 4:35–41, Matthew 8:23–27, Luke 8:22–25

Week 3 – Day Three

Then the Lord sent a great wind on the sea, and such a violent storm arose that the ship threatened to break up. All the sailors were afraid and each cried out to his own god. And they threw the cargo into the sea to lighten the ship.

— *JONAH 1:4–5*

God sent a storm. He was trying to get someone's attention, and that person was Jonah. You may be familiar with the story of Jonah and the whale, but you may have forgotten how it all started.

You see, God gave Jonah a clear commission, "Go to the great city of Nineveh and preach against it, because its wickedness has come up before me." (Jonah 1:2) But Jonah didn't want to go. Instead, he laced up his sandals and took off running—in the opposite direction—to Tarshish! But as he learned—and we all know—you cannot outrun God. When Jonah boarded a boat, God sent a great storm to stop him.

Jonah knew it was his disobedience that had caused his fellow shipmates to now be in danger, so he pleaded for the men to throw him overboard. But before his departure, Jonah made it clear, "I am a Hebrew and I worship the Lord, the God of heaven, who made the sea and the dry land." (Jonah 1:9) Immediately after tossing Jonah into the sea, the raging storm subsided, and all aboard were amazed and made offerings to God. Jonah's words before his seemingly sacrificial death brought every shipmate to the Lord.

And Jonah? Somehow—from out of nowhere—a gigantic fish appeared and swallowed him up. But it didn't kill him. Jonah lived in the belly of that fish for three days and three nights, repenting, praying, and worshipping the Lord. Soon, he was back on dry land and ready to complete God's mission.

QUESTION

Has God ever sent a storm to help you get back on track? Did it impact others around you in a positive or negative way?

PRAYER

Lord, thank you for sending storms to stop us from running from you. Empower us to be obedient so that our actions don't affect others around us in a negative way. Amen.

DIG DEEPER

The Story of Jonah — Jonah 1–4

Week 3 – Day Four

"Therefore, in order to keep me from becoming conceited, I was given a thorn in my flesh, a messenger of Satan, to torment me. Three times I pleaded with the Lord to take it away from me. But he said to me, 'My grace is sufficient for you, for my power is made perfect in weakness.'"

— 2 CORINTHIANS 12:7–9A

Paul had a thorn in his flesh. We don't know what it was, but we know that it was painful—physically, emotionally, or both. That wasn't his only struggle. Out of all the characters in the Bible (besides Jesus, of course), Paul endured more attacks, imprisonments, and persecution for spreading the gospel than anyone else.

After his conversion on the Road to Damascus, the disciples doubted him and the Jews wanted to kill him, but he pushed on with Jesus' mission. He was imprisoned, shipwrecked, under house arrest, and eventually martyred in Rome. Paul met storms throughout his ministry but found joy amidst the most difficult circumstances.

While in prison he wrote a letter to encourage the church in Philippi. In it, his joy is evident, and he found purpose in his pain: "Now I want you to know, brothers and sisters, that what has happened to me has actually served to advance the gospel. As a result, it has become clear throughout the whole palace guard and to everyone else that I am in chains for Christ." (Philippians 1:12–13) While many behind bars would be wallowing in their bondage, Paul was on mission converting the prison guards.

No matter the dire circumstances, Paul forged on trusting the Lord every step of the way. "That is why, for Christ's sake, I delight in weaknesses, in insults, in hardships, in persecutions, in difficulties. For when I am weak, then I am strong." (2 Corinthians 12:10)

QUESTION

Do you have a thorn that has caused great suffering? Like Paul, do you look to the Lord for strength during your storms?

PRAYER

Lord, thank you for Paul's example of joy despite his struggles. Help us to be grateful for our weaknesses, which showcase your strength. Amen.

DIG DEEPER

The Ministry of Paul and His Missionary Journeys — Acts 9–28
(More of Paul's story can be found in his letters to the churches.)

Week 3 – Day Five

*From noon until three in the afternoon darkness came over all
the land. About three in the afternoon Jesus cried out in a loud
voice, "Eli, Eli, lema sabachthani?" (which means "My God,
my God, why have you forsaken me?").*

— MATTHEW 27:45–46

Of all the suffering recorded in the Bible, nothing compares to the
crucifixion of Jesus. As portrayed in the movie, *The Passion of the
Christ*, the gruesome beating, bloody torturing, and unbearable
agony of Jesus is almost too difficult to watch. But Jesus' affliction
didn't only happen at the end of his life. He lived the life of a
suffering servant.

Throughout Jesus' ministry, he was attacked and ridiculed for his
message of forgiveness, peace, and love. His hometown turned their
back on him—even his siblings. His disciples doubted him. One
betrayed him, and another denied him. Religious leaders wanted to
kill him. Jesus knew what it was like to be all alone with the world

against him, even feeling abandoned by his own Father as he took his last breath on the cross.

But, he endured it all for us. His suffering had a purpose—an eternal one. Because Jesus lived, died, and rose again, we too can live with him forever. But it won't be easy.

If we are to follow Jesus, we too will suffer. There will be trials, pain, lost relationships, betrayal by those we love, and death. Jesus knew this and made it clear: "Whoever wants to be my disciple must deny themselves and take up their cross and follow me. For whoever wants to save their life will lose it, but whoever loses their life for me will find it." (Matthew 16:24–25)

QUESTION

Are you willing to follow Jesus at all costs? Will you take up your cross daily to follow him?

PRAYER

Lord, you endured the greatest suffering—for us. Please give us strength to pick up our cross daily to follow you. Amen.

DIG DEEPER

The Crucifixion of Jesus — Matthew 27, Mark 15, Luke 23, John 19

(The life, death, and resurrection of Jesus can be found in the Gospels of Matthew, Mark, Luke, and John.)

Take a Step

Storms. They are a natural part of life. Some we cause. Others just happen. Sometimes Jesus sends them to correct or strengthen us. Other times Satan devises them to derail us. No matter the source, Jesus will be with us through the storms that will inevitably arrive. Jesus sent a squall to strengthen his disciples' faith and also to stop Jonah from fleeing his calling. Paul lived with a thorn in his side and also encountered many trials throughout his ministry. And Jesus, the creator of the storms, carried a cross and died on it for us.

HOW DO YOU HANDLE THE STORMS IN YOUR LIFE? DO YOU FEEL GOD'S PRESENCE WHEN YOU ARE IN THEM?

STEP—What small step can you take today?

TRUST—Will you trust and surrender to the Lord?

ENCOURAGE—Who can encourage you along your journey?

PRAY—Pray for the Lord to give you strength and direct your next steps.

Seek

Shortly before dawn Jesus went out to them, walking on the lake.

— MATTHEW 14:25

Week 4 – Day One

Shortly before dawn Jesus went out to them, walking on the lake.

— MATTHEW 14:25

It was early in the morning when Jesus finished praying. The boat carrying his disciples was already "a considerable distance from land, buffeted by the waves because the wind was against it." (Matthew 14:24) But that did not stop Jesus. The rough waters would not deter him from getting to his beloved believers—nothing would.

Just like the miracle the day before when Jesus turned a few loaves of bread and a couple of fish into a feast for thousands, he walked right to the boat—*on the water*. No storm or waves would get in the way. Jesus made a beeline to his disciples as if the lake were land.

Just like he walked on water to reach his disciples, he will do whatever it takes to reach us, too. Jesus is constantly seeking and pursuing his people, no matter where they are or what the situation may be.

Now he is eager to meet you right where you are—whether it takes a miracle or not. All you need to do is show up with an open heart and mind, trusting that Jesus is with you every step of the way.

QUESTION

Jesus is seeking and pursuing you right now. What is holding you back from receiving all he has to offer?

PRAYER

Lord, thank you for meeting us right where we are. Please remove any barriers that may separate us, even if it takes a miracle. You are the miracle maker! Amen.

Week 4 – Day Two

"What do you think? If a man owns a hundred sheep, and one of them wanders away, will he not leave the ninety-nine on the hills and go to look for the one that wandered off?"

— MATTHEW 18:12

He left the ninety-nine. It doesn't make logical sense to risk the lives of the entire flock for a chance—not a guarantee—of even finding the one sheep that had gone missing. But Jesus' actions don't always make sense to our limited minds. Such is the case with this story of the Parable of the Lost Sheep. What it shows us is that Jesus will go to extreme measures to pursue his children, even in their times of wandering.

You see, our Father never stops seeking and pursuing us. He cares too much, just like a shepherd watching over every last sheep in his flock. He knows there is protection in the pack, especially in our dangerous world. In our times of wandering, when alone and isolated, we are vulnerable—like a sole sheep on the side of a mountain. And just like the shepherd, Jesus risks it all for us.

Jesus never stops pursuing us. And when he finds us, there will be a great celebration. "Truly I tell you, he is happier about that one sheep than about the ninety-nine that did not wander off. In the same way your Father in heaven is not willing that any of these little ones should perish." (Matthew 18:13–14)

QUESTION

Have you wandered away from Jesus? Your church family? Fellow believers? What can you do today to take a step to reconnect?

PRAYER

Lord, thank you for leaving the ninety-nine sheep to come after me, especially in my times of wandering. Help me to stay connected to you and the flock. Amen.

DIG DEEPER

Parable of the Lost Sheep — Matthew 18:10–14

Week 4 – Day Three

Then the man and his wife heard the sound of the Lord God as he was walking in the garden in the cool of the day, and they hid from the Lord God among the trees of the garden. But the Lord God called to the man, "Where are you?"

— GENESIS 3:8–9

Adam and Eve had it made. They were living in paradise—literally— amidst a perfect, lush garden that God had meticulously created just for them. But something went terribly wrong. Eve decided to take hold of the one thing—the *only* thing—that God had told them not to touch. With one bite of enticing fruit, everything changed, not only for the first couple but for all of mankind to come.

You may be familiar with the story known as The Fall, but what happens next may surprise you. God showed up. He took a stroll in the garden seeking Adam and Eve who were now in hiding—feeling exposed and drenched in shame and guilt. In their darkest moment, God was there searching for them.

Of course, there was a consequence for their disobedience, but God also cared for them, "The Lord God made garments of skin for Adam and his wife and clothed them." (Genesis 3:21) God did not abandon Adam and Eve. He was still providing for the first couple and was physically present for them, even after their disobedience.

QUESTION

How has God shown up for you in difficult times when you've made choices outside of his will?

PRAYER

Lord, thank you for showing up and searching us out, even in our times of disobedience. Help us to trust you and not be led astray like Adam and Eve. Amen.

DIG DEEPER

The Fall — Genesis 3

Week 4 – Day Four

When Jesus reached the spot, he looked up and said to him, "Zacchaeus, come down immediately. I must stay at your house today." So he came down at once and welcomed him gladly.

— *LUKE 19:5–6*

He was up in a tree. Not where you would expect to find a wealthy tax collector, but, when Jesus entered Jericho, Zacchaeus' attention was piqued. He wanted to learn more so he raced ahead of the mob and climbed a tree, fearing he would get lost in the crowd below. As he dangled from the branches, little did he know that his life was about to change—for the better.

This wealthy, tree-climbing tax collector was a well-known figure in Jericho—but not a popular one. In those days, tax collectors worked for the Roman government and often padded their own pockets, making the locals despise and consider them thieves. But from all who were present, Jesus picked Zacchaeus out of the masses and invited himself over to his home. While many saw this tax collector as a "sinner," Jesus saw him as a soul in need of saving.

And that's exactly what happened. An encounter with the Lord led to Zacchaeus' repentance. As a result, he repaid the people he had robbed four times the amount stolen from them—to make right his wrongs. And Jesus proclaimed, "Today salvation has come to this house, because this man, too, is a son of Abraham. For the Son of Man came to seek and to save the lost." (Luke 19:9–10)

QUESTION

Zacchaeus was curious about the Lord, and it led to his repentance. Who in your life has a curiosity who you could help lead to the Lord?

PRAYER

Lord, thank you for continuing to seek all people and for planting seeds of curiosity, like you did for Zacchaeus. Open our eyes and hearts to lead others to you. Amen.

DIG DEEPER

Zacchaeus the Tax Collector — Luke 19:1–10

Week 4 – Day Five

But while he was still a long way off, his father saw him and was filled with compassion for him; he ran to his son, threw his arms around him and kissed him.

— LUKE 15:20

He was a long way off, not only in distance but in every way. In the story of the Prodigal Son, the younger son demanded his inheritance and then skipped town. This would have brought immediate humiliation, not only to the father but to the entire family as the younger son was basically declaring, "You are dead to me now." Grief, anger, shame, and guilt would have been this devastated father's expected reaction. But that's not how the story unfolds.

Instead, we see a loving father longing for his ungrateful son's return. No one knows exactly how long he waited, but with each sunrise the father would hope for a glimpse of his beloved on the horizon. Would this be the day of his prodigal's return—or would he ever return? What was he doing in a foreign land? Was he successful? In prison? Or worst case, dead? Questions such as these likely lingered as the days dragged on.

Then one day it happened. The elderly father spotted a figure in the distance. He immediately kicked off his sandals and took off running toward his wayward son. The past did not matter. This devoted dad was grateful his son was alive and back home. His waiting and hoping was worth it.

Now it was time to celebrate: "Quick! Bring the best robe and put it on him. Put a ring on his finger and sandals on his feet. Bring the fattened calf and kill it. Let's have a feast and celebrate. For this son of mine was dead and is alive again; he was lost and is found." (Luke 15:22b–24a)

QUESTION

We all know prodigals and may have even been one at some point in our life. How can we now become more like the father in this story?

PRAYER

Lord, you have unending mercy as you wait for prodigals to return. Thank you for your patience in our times of wandering and disobedience. Empower us to be more like the father. Amen.

DIG DEEPER

The Parable of the Prodigal Son — Luke 15:11–32

Take a Step

Jesus is always seeking and pursuing his children. He walked on water to get to his disciples. He left the ninety-nine to go after the one lost sheep. He searched the Garden of Eden looking for Adam and Eve—even after they disobeyed him. He had dinner with a despised tax collector and waited patiently for the prodigal to return.

Now Jesus is seeking you. Are you ready to receive the abundant life he has to offer to you?

STEP—WHAT SMALL STEP CAN YOU TAKE TODAY?

TRUST—WILL YOU TRUST AND SURRENDER TO THE LORD?

ENCOURAGE—WHO CAN ENCOURAGE YOU ALONG YOUR JOURNEY?

PRAY—PRAY FOR THE LORD TO GIVE YOU STRENGTH AND DIRECT YOUR NEXT STEPS.

Fear

When the disciples saw him walking on the lake, they were terrified.

"It's a ghost," they said, and cried out in fear.

— MATTHEW 14:26

Week 5 – Day One

When the disciples saw him walking on the lake, they were terrified.

"It's a ghost," they said, and cried out in fear.

— MATTHEW 14:26

They did not recognize Jesus. Despite spending many days journeying together and celebrating a huge feast with the masses the day before, the disciples were confused at the person approaching them. Actually, they were terrified! And can you blame them? This man was not in a boat, he was walking *on the water*. Of course, they thought he was a ghost. What was happening right before their eyes was not humanly possible.

Fear. It can paralyze us. It can also blind us. We don't see clearly when despair comes knocking at our door. That's what happened to the disciples on that stormy early morning. They did not recognize Jesus because fear had taken them captive.

The phrase "Fear Not" is one of the most widely used phrases in the Bible—and for good reason. We fear change, health issues, broken relationships, financial instability, career challenges, and especially death. Sometimes fear causes a physiological response—our hearts race, adrenaline rushes, body trembles, or it may even shut down. We likely have heard the terms, "fight, flight, or freeze" which are natural bodily stress responses. What if, in these moments, we pray and talk to God—redirect our focus to him instead of the subject of our fear.

Fight, flight, freeze, or focus? No matter the circumstance, Jesus wants you to trust him and not fear. He is with you when the storms arrive and also in the calm seas. Even when you don't recognize him, he is there.

QUESTION

In our ever-changing world, fear is a common response when unexpected events occur. What are you most fearful of right now?

PRAYER

Lord, we, like the disciples, have moments of fear that blind us. Redirect our focus on you and empower us to pray to overcome our fears so that we may see you clearly. Amen.

Week 5 – Day Two

On the evening of that first day of the week, when the disciples were together, with the doors locked for fear of the Jewish leaders, Jesus came and stood among them and said, "Peace be with you!"

— JOHN 20:19

The disciples were afraid. Of all of the people in the Bible, you would think Jesus' closest companions would be steadfast in their faith. They had been physically with him for years, received daily lessons and one-on-one teaching, and were eye witnesses to numerous healings and miracles. The disciples knew Jesus intimately.

But when times got tough and Jesus was arrested, fear took hold of them. Peter, whose name ironically means "rock," denied Jesus three times. Judas betrayed him for a sack of coins. The rest of the disciples deserted him. Only John remained at the foot of the cross with Mary.

Thankfully, the story doesn't end there. Everything changed after the resurrection. When Jesus appeared out of nowhere behind closed doors, the disciples were given a second chance and a special gift. "He breathed on them and said, 'Receive the Holy Spirit.'" (John 20:22) While Jesus would no longer be physically present to strengthen their faith, he would be living inside of them—empowering them through his Spirit.

And now we, too, have the gift of the Holy Spirit to guide our steps and remind us that God is always with us. There is nothing to fear.

QUESTION

Do you feel the power of the Holy Spirit in your life? How have you been empowered through his Spirit?

PRAYER

Lord, thank you for the gift of your Holy Spirit who lives in us, to guide and empower us to walk in your ways. We have nothing to fear as we know we never walk alone. Amen.

DIG DEEPER

Jesus Appears to His Disciples — John 20:19–29, Matthew 28:16–20, Mark 16:12–20, Luke 24:13–53

The Coming of the Holy Spirit to Believers — Acts 2

Week 5 – Day Three

Elijah was afraid and ran for his life. When he came to Beer-sheba in Judah, he left his servant there, while he himself went a day's journey into the wilderness. He came to a broom bush, sat down under it and prayed that he might die. "I have had enough, Lord," he said. "Take my life; I am no better than my ancestors."

— 1 KINGS 19:3–4

He had just had a mountaintop victory—literally. At Elijah's request, God showed up in a big way, with a blazing fire to showcase his power on Mount Carmel. The people were astonished; they fell to their faces and believed in Elijah's God. The prophets of Baal and Asherah were defeated and eliminated—850 in total! It was truly a victory for God and for the prophet Elijah, but it didn't last for long.

A few verses later we read about how Queen Jezebel was not happy when King Ahab shared the story of her gods' epic defeat. She then sent a message to Elijah with a death threat. She was coming after him. The victorious prophet's response, "Elijah was afraid and ran for his life." What? God's messenger who had just experienced a miraculous event was now running for his life?

This story may seem surprising, but it speaks to the humanness of God's prophets. We have an enemy who is always waiting to move in. Even after our mountaintop experiences, we can have moments of doubt, which can create an opening for fear to take hold.

But God never leaves our side, and he didn't leave Elijah's either. As the story unfolds, an angel of Lord appeared and provided exactly what Elijah needed to strengthen him to continue his ministry.

QUESTION

Have you had a situation in which God showed up in a big way only to be followed by moments of doubt and fear?

PRAYER

Lord, thank you for not only showing up in our mountaintop experiences, but especially in our valleys. Guard our minds to not allow the enemy to plant seeds of doubt or fear. Amen.

DIG DEEPER

Prophet Elijah's Story — 1 Kings 17–21, 2 Kings 1–2

Week 5 – Day Four

"Lord," Ananias answered, "I have heard many reports about this man and all the harm he has done to your holy people in Jerusalem. And he has come here with authority from the chief priests to arrest all who call on your name."

— ACTS 9:13–14

Ananias was afraid. Can you blame him? God's request to go to Saul from Tarsus to restore his sight seemed like an assured death sentence —or at least an immediate arrest. You see, Saul was well known at the time for his goal to stamp out followers of Christ, and he had threatened to murder the disciples. He even had a letter in hand from the high priest to arrest any believers who crossed his path.

Fear. It's a real emotion that happens to all of us—and it happened to Ananias. But often what we fear never happens. A friend once shared a definition of fear as: False Evidence Appearing Real. While fear is a real feeling and reaction, the source of our fear often never comes to fruition. This was the case with Ananias.

As the story continues, we see how this faithful servant did not stay in his fear or allow it to paralyze him from accomplishing God's mission. In fact, although Ananias is only mentioned in a few lines of Scripture, his obedience had a big impact. He did, indeed, do as God commanded, and, during their encounter, Ananias baptized Saul. As a result, Saul (later known as Paul) became one of the greatest apostles of all time.

Sometimes we don't understand God's ways and the seemingly crazy missions he sends us on, but God always has a plan and a purpose. He wanted Ananias to be a part of Saul's conversion then, and he wants us to be a part of his work in the world now.

Question

Has God called you to do something that caused you great fear? Were you able to work through it? What was the result?

Prayer

Lord, sometimes we are afraid. Comfort us so that we don't allow fear to paralyze us. Help us to trust you, especially in those situations that create anxiety. Amen.

Dig Deeper

Saul's Conversion — Acts 9:1–19

Week 5 – Day Five

"Pardon me, my lord," Gideon replied, "but how can I save Israel? My clan is the weakest in Manasseh, and I am the least in my family." The Lord answered, "I will be with you, and you will strike down all the Midianites, leaving none alive." Gideon replied, "If now I have found favor in your eyes, give me a sign that it is really you talking to me."

— JUDGES 6:15–17

Gideon was afraid and questioned the Lord. Could God really want *him* to rescue the Israelites from the oppressive Midianites? Gideon was certainly not equipped and wanted more proof that it was really God speaking, so he asked God for a sign.

Sometimes we're afraid. We want more proof, especially when God asks us to do something that seems impossible. When Gideon asked for a sign, God was patient with him. God made his presence known and then assured Gideon with his comforting words, "Peace! Do not be afraid. You are not going to die." (Judges 6:23)

Although Gideon was initially reluctant and hiding from the Midianites in a winepress, God's presence reassured him and also empowered him to be a great military leader, defeating the Midianite army of 135,000 with a mere 300 men.

Despite his victories, Gideon's need for something tangible to worship "became a snare to Gideon and to his family." Even though Gideon refused to become king at the people's request, he created an ornamental, jeweled robe worn by kings and displayed it in his city for all to see and worship. (Judges 8:27)

When God calls us to a task, he will equip us. And when we succeed, we are to worship our Lord alone and give him all the glory.

QUESTION

Gideon asked for a sign to discern if it was really God speaking. How do you discern God's voice when you question your calling?

PRAYER

Lord, sometimes we're afraid that we don't have what it takes to accomplish your mission. Please comfort us and assure us in these moments so that we may walk in your will. Amen.

DIG DEEPER

Gideon's Story — Judges 6–8

Take a Step

The disciples were afraid. They didn't recognize Jesus when he came walking toward them on the water. Fear blinded them, not only then but many other times throughout Jesus' ministry. In fact, when Jesus needed his disciples the most, they ran in fear. Elijah ran too, but it was in fear of Queen Jezebel's wrath. And then there was Ananias, a faithful follower of Jesus, who was terrified when God asked him to seek out Saul. But Gideon was the most reluctant and fearful of all, known as the poster boy of fear in the Bible. It's interesting to note that the common thread of most of these stories is that fear was caused by other people.

WHAT CAUSES YOU GREAT FEAR? WHAT CAN YOU LEARN FROM THESE STORIES TO HELP YOU CONQUER YOUR FEARS?

STEP—WHAT SMALL STEP CAN YOU TAKE TODAY?

TRUST—WILL YOU TRUST AND SURRENDER TO THE LORD?

ENCOURAGE—WHO CAN ENCOURAGE YOU ALONG YOUR JOURNEY?

PRAY—PRAY FOR THE LORD TO GIVE YOU STRENGTH AND DIRECT YOUR NEXT STEPS.

Courage

But Jesus immediately said to them: "Take courage! It is I. Don't be afraid."

"Lord, if it's you," Peter replied, "tell me to come to you on the water."

— MATTHEW 14:27-28

Week 6 – Day One

But Jesus immediately said to them: "Take courage! It is I. Don't be afraid."

"Lord, if it's you," Peter replied, "tell me to come to you on the water."

— MATTHEW 14:27-28

Take courage! Those were Jesus' words when he saw his terrified disciples as he approached them on the stormy seas. Fear was consuming them. Jesus knew exactly what to say to calm their anxiety, but what did he mean? How do we "Take courage?"

Merriam-Webster defines courage as "mental or moral strength to venture, persevere, and withstand danger, fear, or difficulty." But where does such strength come from? How do we *get* courage? In this story, guidance can be found through the original biblical language. There we discover that this type of courage is infused by God's Spirit. We can't create it on our own—God gives it to us. A Greek word study on *BibleHub* translates "Take courage" as "God bolstering the believer, empowering them with a bold inner-attitude ... it is the result of the Lord infusing his strength by his inworking of faith." (*BibleHub*, https://biblehub.com/greek/2293.htm)

As this story continues, we see how it plays out. With Jesus' words, Peter immediately responds, and his fear subsides. Peter only needed reassurance that the voice he was hearing really was the Lord's.

Throughout the gospels, we see Jesus' presence strengthening his people—and later infusing believers with the Holy Spirit—to overcome fears and accomplish the impossible. On our own strength we will stumble, but as the apostle Paul reminds us, "I can do all things through Christ who strengthens me." (Philippians 4:13 NKJV)

QUESTION

Have you ever felt the Lord strengthen you through a dangerous or difficult situation? What was the result?

PRAYER

Lord, thank you for your strength that emboldens us in times of fear or weakness. Please empower and protect us through our stormy days, and give us your courage. Amen.

Week 6 – Day Two

Then Esther sent this reply to Mordecai: "Go, gather together all the Jews who are in Susa, and fast for me. Do not eat or drink for three days, night or day. I and my attendants will fast as you do. When this is done, I will go to the king, even though it is against the law. And if I perish, I perish."

— ESTHER 4:15-16

It was a life-or-death situation. An edict had been issued for the elimination of the Jewish people, and Queen Esther was the only person in the position to save them. But going to the king unannounced could cost her life. What would she do?

Courage is the word that often comes to mind when we think of Esther. But where did her courage come from? When we read the verses above, we get a glimpse of the answer to this question as we see how Esther prepared for her meeting with the king. She fasted and asked her people to do the same. Then, after days of not eating or drinking she donned her royal robes and approached the king with strength, determination, and wisdom.

The story of Esther is told in the book of the Bible bearing her name. It is the tale of a young Jewish girl raised by her cousin, Mordecai, living in Persia after the Babylonian exile. Esther, a foreigner, eventually becomes queen and saves the Jewish people from an evil plot by Haman, the Persian king's right-hand man. The Book of Esther tells of the deliverance of the Jewish people, and it remains a popular story today—read during the Festival of Purim.

While God is never mentioned by name in this book, he is at work throughout it, placing a young Jewish girl on the throne and empowering her with courage and a plan that eventually saves her people.

QUESTION

Can you look back and see how God has worked behind the scenes to give you strength and wisdom you didn't see at the time?

PRAYER

Lord, thank you for always working on our behalf to accomplish your purposes. Give us the eyes to see you and the strength to empower us, especially when life or death situations arise. Amen.

DIG DEEPER

Esther's story can be found in the Book of Esther.

Week 6 – Day Three

David said to the Philistine, "You come against me with sword and spear and javelin, but I come against you in the name of the Lord Almighty, the God of the armies of Israel, whom you have defied."

— 1 SAMUEL 17:45

David approached the taunting giant with a sling and a stone. That's not all. David had the power of God with him, and he wasn't shy about boldly proclaiming it to the Philistine army that was eagerly awaiting his destruction. But God had a different plan.

You have probably heard the story of David and Goliath. It is a tale with an unlikely hero, a small shepherd boy who showed up on the battlefield with food and provisions for his brothers who, along with their fellow soldiers, were paralyzed in fear of facing the opposing giant. But what they perceived as an immediate death sentence, David saw as an opportunity to showcase God's power.

God not only empowered David with courage but gave him unwavering confidence through real-life preparation, "Your servant has killed both the lion and the bear; this uncircumcised Philistine will be like one of them, because he has defied the armies of the living God. The Lord who rescued me from the paw of the lion and the paw of the bear will rescue me from the hand of this Philistine." (1 Samuel 17:36-37a)

With neither armor nor sword in hand, but with the faith of a giant, God gave his faithful servant David a miraculous victory. And, as his story unfolds, David becomes one of the greatest kings of Israel, forever known as "A man after God's own heart." (Acts 13:22)

QUESTION

Have you, like David, seized an opportunity to showcase God's power when others were fearful? What was the result?

PRAYER

Lord, thank you for David's story of how you equip us for any task you call us to do. Help us to lean into your power when fear or anxiety sets in. Give us the faith of a giant. Amen.

DIG DEEPER

Story of David and Goliath — 1 Samuel 17

Week 6 – Day Four

"Be strong and very courageous. Be careful to obey all the law my servant Moses gave you; do not turn from it to the right or to the left, that you may be successful wherever you go."

— JOSHUA 1:7

Finally, the time had come. The Israelites were ready to take control of the land that God had promised their ancestor Abraham over 400 years earlier. (Genesis 15:13) But it would not be easy. The land was occupied by other tribes, and they would not leave without a fight. Their faithful leader Moses had died, and God had chosen Joshua to now lead the conquest of the Promised Land.

The Book of Joshua begins with God guiding his new leader on the difficult task ahead. After outlining the boundaries of the Israelites' new territory, God repeats several times, "Be strong and courageous. Do not be afraid." God not only affirms that he will be with them through these battles, but he provides Joshua with specific instructions: "Keep this Book of the Law always on your lips; meditate on it day and night, so that you may be careful to do everything written in it. Then you will be prosperous and successful." (Joshua 1:8) God's presence and Word were all that they needed to succeed.

And indeed they did! Joshua did exactly what God instructed, and their first conquest was an undeniable success. After marching around Jericho for six days, on the seventh day they circled seven times and—with the blow of the rams' horns and a loud shout—the walls fell and the city was conquered!

God empowered Joshua and his army through his Word and his promised presence. God is doing the same for us today.

QUESTION

When conflict is on the horizon, how do you prepare for the encounter? How has God helped you conquer your battles?

PRAYER

Lord, thank you for always being with us and for giving us guidance through your Word. Help us to be obedient to you, as Joshua was. Amen.

DIG DEEPER

Moses' Successor, Blessing, and Death — Deuteronomy 31–34
Joshua's Commission by God and the Conquering of Jericho — Joshua 1–6

Week 6 – Day Five

Shadrach, Meshach and Abednego replied to him, "King Nebuchadnezzar, we do not need to defend ourselves before you in this matter. If we are thrown into the blazing furnace, the God we serve is able to deliver us from it, and he will deliver us from Your Majesty's hand. But even if he does not, we want you to know, Your Majesty, that we will not serve your gods or worship the image of gold you have set up."

— DANIEL 3:16–18

The fire was blazing hot. In fact, when Shadrach, Meshach, and Abednego would not bow down to worship the king's golden image, he was so angry that he "ordered the furnace heated seven times hotter than usual." (Daniel 3:19b) The heat was so scorching that the soldiers who tied up and threw God's faithful servants into the fire died from the intense flames. How could anyone survive?

Not only did these three devoted Jews in Babylon prevail, they were soon unbound and walking around in the fiery furnace! And they were not alone. Suddenly, another figure appeared in the fire with them who looked like "a son of the gods." (Daniel 3:25) Many biblical scholars believe it was Jesus by their side, protecting them and leaving the king and all present in wonder and awe.

When the three emerged from the furnace unharmed—without a scent of fire on them—the king was amazed. He proclaimed, "Praise be to the God of Shadrach, Meshach and Abednego, who has sent his angel and rescued his servants! They trusted in him and defied the king's command and were willing to give up their lives rather than serve or worship any god except their own God." (Daniel 3:28)

Their courage in the face of a deadly inferno—grounded in their unwavering faith—showcased the power of the one true God.

QUESTION

Has your faith ever been publicly tested? How did you respond? What was the result?

PRAYER

Lord, thank you for empowering us when we need courage, just like you did for Shadrach, Meshach, and Abednego. Embolden us to declare our faith in you when put to the test. Amen.

DIG DEEPER

Story of Shadrach, Meshach, and Abednego — Daniel 1–3

Take a Step

Courage. It's not a natural reaction. When fearful situations arise, most of us don't suddenly become courageous. We need the Lord to empower us. Esther's life was on the line, and she fasted and asked her people to join her. After days without food or drink, God empowered her to go to the king. David was fearless when he approached the colossal giant Goliath, and then he killed him with a small stone. Joshua leaned on the Lord for strength and guidance, and the walls of Jericho miraculously collapsed with the blow of a horn and a shout. Shadrach, Meshach, and Abednego did not flinch at the site of a deadly fire and walked in the flames with the Lord.

HOW CAN THESE BIBLICAL HEROES EMPOWER YOU TO CONQUER YOUR GIANTS—NOT WITH YOUR OWN POWER BUT WITH GOD'S?

STEP—WHAT SMALL STEP CAN YOU TAKE TODAY?

TRUST—WILL YOU TRUST AND SURRENDER TO THE LORD?

ENCOURAGE—WHO CAN ENCOURAGE YOU ALONG YOUR JOURNEY?

PRAY—PRAY FOR THE LORD TO GIVE YOU STRENGTH AND DIRECT YOUR NEXT STEPS.

Invite

"Come," he said.

— MATTHEW 14:29A

Week 7 – Day One

"Come," he said.

— MATTHEW 14:29A

Jesus invited Peter to come out of the boat. It was a personal appeal to join him on the turbulent water. It was not an invitation to join him in the sunny meadows on a beautiful, blue-sky day. They were in the midst of a torrential downpour. The waves were threatening. The skies were thundering. Peter could drown. What kind of invitation was this?

At the surface, Jesus' invitation may not make sense. But this calling was not about an event or the circumstances, it was about trust. Jesus was drawing Peter out into the deep, dark waters to join him in the storm. It would be much easier and safer to make this request with clear skies above. In turbulent times, stepping out into the unknown requires faith and trust in the Lord. And, in that moment, Peter had it.

Jesus invites us to join him, too. Sometimes he calls us into difficult situations and life-threatening circumstances. But, just like with Peter, Jesus is asking us to trust that he will be there with us every step of the stormy way.

And if we become overwhelmed or burned out, he invites us to be renewed in him. "Come to me, all you who are weary and burdened, and I will give you rest. Take my yoke upon you and learn from me, for I am gentle and humble in heart, and you will find rest for your souls." (Matthew 11:28–29)

Whether bright skies or dreary days, we never walk alone.

QUESTION

Has the Lord called you into a difficult situation? How did you respond? What happened as a result?

PRAYER

Lord, sometimes you call us into storms, but it's always with a purpose. In those times, help us to trust you and know that you are walking with us. Amen.

Week 7 – Day Two

As Jesus was walking beside the Sea of Galilee, he saw two brothers, Simon called Peter and his brother Andrew. They were casting a net into the lake, for they were fishermen. "Come, follow me," Jesus said, "and I will send you out to fish for people." At once they left their nets and followed him.

— MATTHEW 4:18–20

Follow me. These two words changed Peter and Andrew's lives—forever. With this invitation, Jesus was not only calling them to join his mission, he was offering them a life of transformation. This was only the beginning of Jesus gathering together an unlikely group of common people to change the world.

What may be surprising is that they immediately dropped their nets to follow Jesus. They were not only abandoning their jobs but leaving their families, their livelihood, and their source of support for their loved ones. They were giving up everything to follow Jesus—and they did it without pause.

We, too, are given that same opportunity. Jesus invites every single person on earth to follow him. He does not compel or force anyone. With his words, "Come, follow me," Jesus welcomes us to walk with him, to abide in his ways and teachings, and to seek a personal relationship with him for eternity.

But many reject Jesus' offer. Our world entices and pulls us away, tempting us with material things or worldly ways that are more alluring in the moment. Still Jesus waits patiently, and his invitation is available any time and to anyone.

QUESTION

Have you accepted Jesus' invitation to follow him into a new life? If not, what is your hesitation? Is there an obstacle?

PRAYER

Lord, thank you for your gracious and loving invitation to follow you. Help us to respond as the disciples did—fully committing our lives to you. Amen.

DIG DEEPER

"Follow Me" — Jesus spoke these words 21 times in 12 different conversations in the gospels. Here are a few examples: Matthew 4:19, Mark 1:17, Matthew 8:22, Matthew 9:9, Mark 2:14, Luke 5:27, John 1:43, John 12:26, Luke 9:59.

Week 7 – Day Three

Then, leaving her water jar, the woman went back to the town and said to the people, "Come, see a man who told me everything I ever did. Could this be the Messiah?" They came out of the town and made their way toward him.

— JOHN 4:28–30

It was a divine encounter in the middle of the day. Jesus' conversation with an unnamed woman at Jacob's well may not appear to be a big deal until we dig deeper into the story.

You see, this woman was a Samaritan. Since the Assyrian conquest of the Northern Kingdom of Israel around 722 B.C., the Samaritans were despised by the Jewish people and considered a mixed breed. Jews would intentionally avoid the region, but as the text reveals, "he *had* to go through Samaria." (John 4:4) Jesus was on a mission with a God-ordained appointment at this particular well with a woman who desperately needed what Jesus had to offer—his living water.

Although she was reluctant and confused at the beginning of their encounter, this broken woman soon realized that the thirsty man before her was not like other Jews. He knew all about her—intimately. He knew that, because of her embarrassment and shame, she was fetching water alone in the middle of the scorching, hot day to avoid facing others. He knew of her many husbands and indiscretions. And mostly, he knew exactly what she needed.

As their conversation continued, her eyes slowly opened, and her curiosity and questioning led to a life-changing revelation. This stranger was the the long-awaited Messiah! The moment Jesus' identity became clear, she dropped her water jug and immediately took off running to tell everyone in town.

QUESTION

Have you had an encounter with Jesus that you couldn't wait to share? Do you openly tell others about your "God Moments?"

PRAYER

Lord, thank you for meeting us exactly where we are, like you did with the woman at the well. Empower us to share our God encounters to help bring others closer to you. Amen.

DIG DEEPER

Jesus Meets the Samaritan Woman at the Well — John 4:1-42

Week 7 – Day Four

Philip found Nathanael and told him, "We have found the one Moses wrote about in the Law, and about whom the prophets also wrote—Jesus of Nazareth, the son of Joseph."

"Nazareth! Can anything good come from there?" Nathanael asked. "Come and see," said Philip.

— JOHN 1:45–46

Philip had just been called by Jesus to follow him. Immediately, this newest recruit enthusiastically set out in search of Nathanael to share the incredible news. But Nathanael didn't have quite the same response nor excitement. Hearing that Jesus was from Nazareth, Nathanael quickly concluded that he could not possibly be the long-awaited Messiah. In response, Philip didn't try to persuade his doubting friend; he simply offered an invitation, "Come and see."

That's the same invitation that Jesus extends to us today—and he wants us to share it with others. In fact, Jesus' final instructions before his ascension to heaven are known as the Great Commission.

(Matthew 28:18–20) In it, we are called to "Go and make disciples" —and it all starts with an invitation.

"Come and see." These three simple words will have a life-changing impact on all who accept the invitation. Now it's our turn to extend it to others.

QUESTION

Who in your life has Jesus nudged you to share his invitation, "Come and see?"

PRAYER

Lord, thank you for the people in our lives who invited us to come and see what you are all about. Please reveal to us who we should now invite to meet you. Amen.

DIG DEEPER

Jesus Calls Philip and Nathanael — John 1:43–51

Week 7 – Day Five

Then he said to them all: "Whoever wants to be my disciple must deny themselves and take up their cross daily and follow me. For whoever wants to save their life will lose it, but whoever loses their life for me will save it."

— LUKE 9:23–24

The cross. It's displayed front and center in churches, hung on chains around necks, staked along roadsides, and marked in ashes on foreheads. When we think of this holy symbol, we likely picture Jesus' lifeless body hanging on it. And through his words, Jesus reminds us that to accept the invitation to follow him means that we, too, will have a cross to bear. To be a true disciple of Jesus will mean that we will suffer as Jesus did.

This may not be what you thought you signed up for when you first became a Christian. But as the years pass and we mature in our walk with Jesus, it becomes painfully clear that life is not easy. A dismal diagnosis arrives, finances become tight, marriages are broken, loved ones are lost. Jesus knew our lives would be difficult. And, out of his great love and mercy for us, he made it clear what following him would require. Jesus was telling us the truth.

He was also providing assurance. Although we would encounter difficulties and inevitable sacrifice and suffering on his behalf, we would ultimately have salvation and eternal life. As the saying goes, "We will have temporary pain for long-term gain."

QUESTION

What cross do you carry daily to follow Jesus? How have you endured it?

PRAYER

Lord, thank you for always telling us the truth, even though it's sometimes difficult to hear. Give us strength to carry our cross wherever you send us. Amen.

DIG DEEPER

The Cost to Follow Jesus — Luke 9:21–27, Matthew 16:21–28, Mark 8:31–38

Take a Step

Come and see. These words had an eternal impact. In the beginning of Jesus' ministry, he made an appeal to his disciples to follow him, one by one, into a new life with him. Jesus later invited Peter to trust him to walk on water through a storm. His invitation was not only for the disciples but for everyone, and he wants us to now extend it to others, as the Samaritan woman and Philip did. With his words "Follow Me," Jesus not only welcomes us into a personal relationship with him, but he invites us to share in his suffering—to carry our cross as he did.

Your relationship with Jesus likely started with an invitation by someone, and now we have an opportunity to pay it forward. What are your obstacles in inviting others to "Come and see?"

STEP—WHAT SMALL STEP CAN YOU TAKE TODAY?

TRUST—WILL YOU TRUST AND SURRENDER TO THE LORD?

ENCOURAGE—WHO CAN ENCOURAGE YOU ALONG YOUR JOURNEY?

PRAY—PRAY FOR THE LORD TO GIVE YOU STRENGTH AND DIRECT YOUR NEXT STEPS.

Obedience

Then Peter got down out of the boat, walked on the water and came toward Jesus.

— MATTHEW 14:29B

Week 8 – Day One

Then Peter got down out of the boat, walked on the water and came toward Jesus.

— MATTHEW 14:29B

He walked on water. When we think of this story, it is likely Jesus who comes to mind. But this time it was Peter! Because he obeyed Jesus, he experienced his own miracle moment.

When I read this passage, the first part jumps out, "Peter got down out of the boat." What if he stayed in the boat? It was safe. There was a gaping abyss that stood between him and Jesus. The boat provided protection against the beating waves. Who would blame Peter for staying in the boat? None of the other disciples moved.

With Jesus' invitation "Come," Peter immediately stepped out and walked on the raging sea toward his Savior. Peter's faith ushered in a miracle—and it started with a decision. He had to take that first step of obedience.

If we desire to follow Jesus, obedience to the Lord's calling will be a daily decision. Just like Peter, we will be called to step out of our comfort zones—and it won't be easy. The boat is comfortable, familiar, and safe. Stepping out in faith is scary and can be filled with many unknowns and turbulent waves to conquer. It's easier to stay where we are.

But God has a much better and bigger plan for our lives. Just like Peter, we have to take that first step. And when we do, Jesus will be right there with us. Our miracle moment awaits!

QUESTION

When God calls you out of your comfort zone, what is your initial reaction? What do you need to do (or stop doing) to be obedient to God's calling?

PRAYER

Lord, we like to be comfortable and safe. Empower us—like Peter—to be obedient when you call us out of our comfort zones and into the unknown. Amen.

Week 8 – Day Two

"How will this be," Mary asked the angel, "since I am a virgin?" The angel answered, "The Holy Spirit will come on you, and the power of the Most High will overshadow you. So the holy one to be born will be called the Son of God. Even Elizabeth your relative is going to have a child in her old age, and she who was said to be unable to conceive is in her sixth month. For no word from God will ever fail." "I am the Lord's servant," Mary answered. "May your word to me be fulfilled." Then the angel left her.

— LUKE 1:34–38

The Virgin Mary. She is revered in many Christian denominations and is highly regarded for her devotion and trust in the Lord. As a young girl (likely 13–15 years old), she was the ultimate example of obedience and faith. Not only was she pregnant out of wedlock, but she would be birthing the Son of God through a divine conception. That would be *a lot* for anyone to take in—especially a teenager!

But God knew exactly who to choose to fulfill his plan. He needed someone with a willing heart and obedient spirit—actually two people were required. Despite Mary being pregnant before their marriage with a baby that was not his own, Joseph took her to be his wife after an angel appeared to him in a dream. God knew that young Mary could not raise this child alone and chose Joseph as Jesus' earthly father.

From the initial angelic proclamations to announce God's sacred plan through their difficult journey to Bethlehem and beyond, this holy couple was obedient to God every step of the way—even when faced with the impossible.

QUESTION

When has God asked you to do something that seemed impossible? How did you respond? What was the result?

PRAYER

Lord, you know exactly what to do and who to choose to accomplish your purposes. Strengthen us to be obedient to your calling, even when it seems impossible. Amen.

DIG DEEPER

The Birth of Jesus Foretold to Mary — Luke 1:26–38
The Birth of Jesus Foretold to Joseph — Matthew 1:18–25

Week 8 – Day Three

Now the earth was corrupt in God's sight and was full of violence. God saw how corrupt the earth had become, for all the people on earth had corrupted their ways. So God said to Noah, "I am going to put an end to all people, for the earth is filled with violence because of them. I am surely going to destroy both them and the earth. So make yourself an ark of cypress wood; make rooms in it and coat it with pitch inside and out."

— *GENESIS* 6:11–14

He built a boat. This may not seem like anything out of the ordinary, but there was no flood—or even rain—at the time. And it was a *big* boat (longer than a football field!) to hold two of every kind of living creature in the world. Everything and everyone else would be wiped out—humans, animals, plants, all living things. God was ushering in the ultimate restart of the world, and Noah and his family would be the sole survivors as "Noah found favor in the eyes of the Lord." (Genesis 6:8)

Most of us know the story of Noah and the Ark. It's a popular childhood tale, and it gives us yet another example of an unlikely character whose obedience was noticed and awarded by God. In fact, it saved his life—and his loved ones too. Throughout the story of Noah building the ark, entering it, and enduring the year-long voyage with a great flood that lasted 150 days after 40 days and nights of rain, there is a common theme and repeated line, "Noah did everything just as God commanded him." (Genesis 6:22)

One man's obedience made a new world possible, and his actions had a ripple effect on us today. Because of Noah's faithfulness, God promised never to destroy the world again through a flood and then established a covenant with Noah, symbolized with a rainbow.

QUESTION

Our lives affect others, just like Noah's did for us today. When has your obedience (or lack of it) had a ripple effect on someone else— positive or negative?

PRAYER

Lord, thank you for your beautiful creation, sealed with a covenant by a rainbow. Help us to be obedient, as Noah was, especially with choices that affect others. Amen.

DIG DEEPER

Noah's Story — Genesis 5–9

Week 8 – Day Four

Hezekiah trusted in the Lord, the God of Israel. There was no one like him among all the kings of Judah, either before him or after him. He held fast to the Lord and did not stop following him; he kept the commands the Lord had given Moses. And the Lord was with him; he was successful in whatever he undertook. He rebelled against the king of Assyria and did not serve him.

— 2 KINGS 18:5–7

Of all the kings in the Bible, Hezekiah was one of the most faithful. "He did what was right in the eyes of the Lord, just as his father David had done." (2 Kings 18:3) When he became king of Judah at the age of 25, he immediately removed idols to false gods, cut down Asherah poles (i.e. sacred tree/pole to a pagan goddess), and purified and repaired the temple. He remained faithful to the Lord even with ominous threats from Assyrian King Sennacherib.

Along with his works of faith that were evident to all, Hezekiah may best be known as a man of prayer. When a defeat by the hands of the

Assyrian king seemed inevitable, King Hezekiah went to the temple to pray. "It is true, Lord, that the Assyrian kings have laid waste these nations and their lands. They have thrown their gods into the fire and destroyed them, for they were not gods but only wood and stone, fashioned by human hands. Now, Lord our God, deliver us from his hand, so that all the kingdoms of the earth may know that you alone, Lord, are God." (2 Kings 19:17–19) God answered his prayer, and 185,000 Assyrian soldiers were found dead the next day. The king retreated and was later killed by his own sons.

Hezekiah's obedience to the Lord was rewarded not only with protection from his enemies but later with a miraculous healing from a deadly illness, extending his life 15 years.

QUESTION

Have you ever felt God's protection or favor while walking in obedience with him?

PRAYER

Lord, thank you for your servant, Hezekiah, who was faithful and trusted you in the face of impossible odds. Help us to follow his example of obedience and prayer. Amen.

DIG DEEPER

Hezekiah's story — 2 Kings 18–20, 2 Chronicles 29–32, Isaiah 36–39

Week 8 – Day Five

He withdrew about a stone's throw beyond them, knelt down and prayed, "Father, if you are willing, take this cup from me; yet not my will, but yours be done." An angel from heaven appeared to him and strengthened him. And being in anguish, he prayed more earnestly, and his sweat was like drops of blood falling to the ground.

— LUKE 22:41–44

Of all the examples of obedience in the Bible, no one can compare to Jesus. When he knew his death was imminent and suffering was upon him, he prayed for deliverance—but with a caveat—only if it was his Father's will. While crying out to God in agony, an angel appeared to give Jesus strength, and he forged on in prayer as his sweat turned to blood.

That was just the beginning. Jesus was obedient through physical torturing, flogging, and later crucifixion. We feel his agony through his own final words, "My God, My God why have you forsaken me?"

(Matthew 27:46) Jesus was fully God but also fully human and could feel the pain with every agonizing strike and each nail driven into his hands. Although he cried out to his Father in distress, Jesus never denied him, even after being tormented by a criminal hanging next to him. Jesus knew where he was going and that his pain had a purpose —our salvation.

Although there are martyrs today around the world dying for their faith, our obedience likely will not cost us our lives. But it will cost us something. If we are to follow Jesus, we are to walk in obedience, as he walked, and pick up our cross daily.

QUESTION

What has obedience to God's calling cost you?

PRAYER

Lord, words cannot describe our gratitude for your ultimate sacrifice for us. Despite the agony and physical torture, you remained obedient to death to save us from our sins. Empower us to pick up our cross daily to follow you. Amen.

DIG DEEPER

Trial, Crucifixion, and Death of Jesus — Matthew 27, Mark 15, Luke 22:66–23:56, John 18:28–19:42

Take a Step

Obedience. It's not a word we like. We fight it as a child and resist it as adults. Being obedient is hard and will likely cost us something. It cost Jesus his life. Mary ended up pregnant and on the run with her young husband Joseph. Only Noah survived being isolated in a boat for 370 days—with his family and lots of animals! Hezekiah endured threats on his life through battles and health issues. Being obedient to the Lord is not easy, but it's worth it.

Do you struggle with obedience to the Lord's calling in your life? What are the obstacles? How can these stories encourage you?

STEP—WHAT SMALL STEP CAN YOU TAKE TODAY?

TRUST—WILL YOU TRUST AND SURRENDER TO THE LORD?

ENCOURAGE—WHO CAN ENCOURAGE YOU ALONG YOUR JOURNEY?

PRAY—PRAY FOR THE LORD TO GIVE YOU STRENGTH AND DIRECT YOUR NEXT STEPS.

Focus

But when he saw the wind, he was afraid and, beginning to sink, cried out, "Lord, save me!"

— MATTHEW 14:30

Week 9 – Day One

But when he saw the wind, he was afraid and, beginning to sink, cried out, "Lord, save me!"

— MATTHEW 14:30

Peter walked on water—at least for a moment, that is. Everything seemed to be going miraculously right. As his feet touched the sea it was as if it had immediately turned to land as he glided on top of it. But then he went down—fast. So, what happened as Peter beelined toward Jesus? In this verse we discover the answer.

"But when he saw the wind, he was afraid." Peter took his focus off of Jesus and onto the storm around him. Fear set in as he looked down at the raging waves at his heels—and he immediately descended into the deep, turbulent waters.

We all have storms in life, and how we endure them depends on where we focus. Are we looking to Jesus or are we distracted by the circumstances around us? As we learn from this story, we need to direct our attention to Jesus, but not only during challenging times. Our focus needs to remain on what's above instead of what's around us each and every day so we don't get distracted and allow fear or doubt to set in.

And if we do, when the storm inevitably arrives we will be walking with Jesus through it, instead of plummeting on our own, in despair.

QUESTION

With what challenge do you face right now do you need to focus on Jesus and his power instead of the circumstances around you?

PRAYER

Lord, thank you for being with us in our storms. Help us to keep our eyes on you instead of what's happening around us. Give us a steadfast focus on you. Amen.

Week 9 – Day Two

But Martha was distracted by all the preparations that had to be made. She came to him and asked, "Lord, don't you care that my sister has left me to do the work by myself? Tell her to help me!"

— *LUKE* 10:40

Martha was in preparation mode. Can you blame her? Jesus and his disciples were in her living room. I can only imagine how I would be scurrying about—furiously cleaning, searching for my best recipes, fluffing pillows—making sure everything was perfect as the long-awaited Messiah walked through the door.

But not Mary. Martha's sister didn't seem to be concerned at all. She had one focus, and it had nothing to do with the condition of their home or the food that would be served. She was sitting at Jesus' feet, soaking in everything he was saying. Mary would not miss a word.

The contrast between these two sisters is obvious. I must confess that I tend to sympathize with Martha—the doer, the one who gets thing done! I would be right by her side with a mop in hand making everything sparkle. And I'm pretty sure I would also speak up with utter dismay as Martha did, appealing to the Lord for Mary's help.

In his gentle wisdom, Jesus responded and made it clear to Martha—and to us—which example to follow, "Martha, Martha," the Lord answered, "you are worried and upset about many things, but few things are needed—or indeed only one. Mary has chosen what is better, and it will not be taken away from her." (Luke 10:41–42)

Jesus is the One. Spending time with Jesus is where our attention should be. Mary made the better choice. She was single-mindedly focused on being in the presence of Jesus. Nothing else mattered.

QUESTION

What distractions do you face in the daily minutiae of life that take your focus away from spending time with Jesus? How can you refocus on the Lord?

PRAYER

Lord, we are distracted with all that's around us—our homes, jobs, and relationships. Thank you for this reminder that you are what's most important. Help us to be more like Mary. Amen.

DIG DEEPER

The Story of Mary and Martha — Luke 10:38–42

Week 9 – Day Three

But Ruth replied, "Don't urge me to leave you or to turn back from you. Where you go I will go, and where you stay I will stay. Your people will be my people and your God my God. Where you die I will die, and there I will be buried. May the Lord deal with me, be it ever so severely, if even death separates you and me."

— RUTH 1:16–17

Ruth was faithful to Naomi. When she remained by Naomi's side, it was more than a decision, she was choosing a new way of life—including home, faith, and family. Despite losing her husband, Ruth's focus was not on herself or what would be best for her own future. Her thoughts and actions were solely centered on Naomi.

This was not an easy choice. You see, in those days, the future of a widow was not promising. Widows were often destitute and relied on family or the community to support them. Not only was Ruth a widow, but, by following Naomi, she would become a foreigner.

This decision would take her from her homeland in Moab to an unknown new beginning in Bethlehem. But she did it anyway.

As the story continues, we see how Ruth's selfless service and love for her mother-in-law led her to God's favor. While gleaning in a field for food, she met the owner Boaz who was immediately smitten, not only with her beauty but her hard work and heart for others. As a result, this impoverished Moabite widow became Boaz's wife, and they became the great grandparents of King David and a part of the lineage of Jesus. (Matthew 1:5-6) Through this unlikely couple, God was at work preparing for future kings.

And it all started with a decision to live a life beyond herself.

QUESTION

When trials arrive, do you focus on yourself and your circumstances or look for opportunities to serve others as Ruth did?

PRAYER

Lord, thank you for this story of a selfless widow who focused on her mother-in-law instead of herself. Open our eyes and heart to serve others as Ruth did. Amen.

DIG DEEPER

Ruth's story can be found in the Book of Ruth.

Week 9 – Day Four

Now this was John's testimony when the Jewish leaders in Jerusalem sent priests and Levites to ask him who he was. He did not fail to confess, but confessed freely, "I am not the Messiah."

— *JOHN 1:19–20*

They thought John the Baptist was the long-awaited Messiah. He was freely baptizing people and proclaiming repentance to all who passed. Jewish leaders continued to question John about his identity, "Who are you? Give us an answer to take back to those who sent us. What do you say about yourself?" (John 1:22) It would have been easy for John the Baptist to claim the title, but he knew who he was —and who he was not.

He also knew his purpose. "I am the voice of one calling in the wilderness, 'Make straight the way for the Lord.'" (John 1:23) John was focused on pointing people to the real Messiah and proclaiming repentance and baptism for the forgiveness of sins. He was not at all interested in drawing attention to himself, although his behavior and bold proclamations often resulted in it. And he was also not shy about calling people out, even taunting the Pharisees as a "brood of vipers." (Matthew 3:7)

When John did come face to face with the true Messiah, he humbled himself and responded, "I need to be baptized by you, and do you come to me?" (Matthew 3:14)

Although John's life was short, his goal was to elevate Jesus and fulfill his purpose to point people to the only one worthy of being called the Messiah.

QUESTION

Does your life point people to Jesus or do you instead seek to draw attention to yourself?

PRAYER

Lord, thank you for John the Baptist who knew who he was and who he wasn't. Empower us to point people to you in all that we do and give you the glory. Amen.

DIG DEEPER

John the Baptist's Ministry — John 1:6–37, Matthew 3, Luke 3:1–20, Mark 1:1–15

Week 9 – Day Five

One evening David got up from his bed and walked around on the roof of the palace. From the roof he saw a woman bathing. The woman was very beautiful, and David sent someone to find out about her. The man said, "She is Bathsheba, the daughter of Eliam and the wife of Uriah the Hittite." Then David sent messengers to get her. She came to him, and he slept with her. Then she went back home. The woman conceived and sent word to David, saying, "I am pregnant."

— 2 SAMUEL 11:2–5

He spotted her from the palace roof one lonely evening. Her body must have been shimmering in the sunset as his glance turned into a stare. The king then had his messengers bring the woman he was admiring from afar into his quarters. What started as a temptation in the distance ended in an illegitimate child. And, as the story unfolds, it becomes even more shocking. King David plots the murder of Bathsheba's husband so he could take her as his wife.

We all have temptations, as King David did with Bathsheba. What we take in through our eyes affects our actions. Just ask Eve, who was tempted by and gave into the fruit that was "pleasing to the eye." (Genesis 3:6) Temptations abound in our world today that steal our focus from the Lord. The challenge is to recognize and avoid them since it's a slippery slope, as David discovered.

What we focus on matters. To keep our gaze on the Lord, Scripture tells us to "Flee the evil desires of youth and pursue righteousness, faith, love, and peace ..." (2 Timothy 2:22a) while "Fixing our eyes on Jesus, the pioneer and perfecter of faith." (Hebrews 12:2a)

Flee and focus. This will take intentional effort and prayer-filled dedication to keep our eyes on the Lord and away from what is not pleasing to him. It's simple, but not easy.

QUESTION

Temptation surrounds us and can hijack God's best for our lives. What do you need to flee that distracts your focus from the Lord?

PRAYER

Lord, we are constantly being lured away from your best, just as David was on the rooftop. Help us to keep our focus steadfast on you. Amen.

DIG DEEPER

Story of David and Bathsheba — 2 Samuel 11:1–12:31

Take a Step

Focus. Peter was walking on water until he took his eyes off of Jesus. He got distracted and sank into the deep waters. Martha was busy preparing for her special guest instead of following Mary's lead of just being present. Ruth did not ruminate on her dire circumstances as a widow, but she was solely concerned with the care and well-being of her mother-in-law. John the Baptist attracted attention as he wandered the countryside, but he always pointed to Jesus instead of promoting himself. David caught a glimpse of a beautiful woman on a rooftop and fell into sin with generational consequences.

WHERE IS YOUR FOCUS TODAY? IS IT ON JESUS AND HIS WILL FOR YOUR LIFE, OR ARE YOU DISTRACTED WITH THE CIRCUMSTANCES AND STORMS AROUND YOU?

STEP—WHAT SMALL STEP CAN YOU TAKE TODAY?

TRUST—WILL YOU TRUST AND SURRENDER TO THE LORD?

ENCOURAGE—WHO CAN ENCOURAGE YOU ALONG YOUR JOURNEY?

PRAY—PRAY FOR THE LORD TO GIVE YOU STRENGTH AND DIRECT YOUR NEXT STEPS.

Rescue

Immediately Jesus reached out his hand and caught him. "You of little faith," he said, "why did you doubt?"

— MATTHEW 14:31

Week 10 – Day One

Immediately Jesus reached out his hand and caught him. "You of little faith," he said, "why did you doubt?"

— MATTHEW 14:31

Peter was given a lifeline. As he plunged into the depths of the stormy sea, a hand reached out. It was Jesus, of course, perfectly positioned for the dramatic rescue. While saving Peter's life may not be surprising, Jesus' response may have been. Instead of consoling his shaken disciple, Jesus rebuked Peter for his lack of faith.

Despite Jesus standing firmly on the violent waves directly in front of him, when Peter's eyes shifted from his Savior to the surrounding storms, fear immediately engulfed him. As his faith began to plummet, so did his body.

When I think of the opposite meaning of faith, the word "fear" usually comes to mind. Just like what happened with Peter, fear can take hold quickly when our faith wanes. But this story reminds us that Jesus is always with us, especially in the midst of our storms. He is also merciful when we, like Peter, have our moments of doubt, and he reaches out to rescue, console, or comfort us. As followers of Jesus, we have nothing to fear.

Jesus is in the business of rescuing his wayward people. His greatest rescue mission came at the cost of his own life as he hung on a cross to free us from the bondage of our sins. There's no greater rescue story than that!

QUESTION

Have you been in a situation where you were overwhelmed and the Lord came to your rescue? What happened?

PRAYER

Lord, thank you for sending a lifeline to rescue us when circumstances drown us and fear sets in. We know that no matter the storm, you are always with us. Amen.

Week 10 – Day Two

Moses stretched out his hand over the sea, and at daybreak the sea went back to its place. The Egyptians were fleeing toward it, and the Lord swept them into the sea. The water flowed back and covered the chariots and horsemen—the entire army of Pharaoh that had followed the Israelites into the sea. Not one of them survived.

— EXODUS 14:27–28

The picture has remained in my mind. Moses, played by Charlton Heston, stretches out his arms wide with staff in hand and declares, "The Lord of hosts will do battle for us. Behold his mighty hand," as the Red Sea parts, creating dry land for the Israelites to safely cross. It's one of the most powerful and dramatic rescue operations in the Bible and now on our screens through the classic movie, *The Ten Commandments*. God protected his people and destroyed the enemy. "And when the Israelites saw the mighty hand of the Lord displayed against the Egyptians, the people feared the Lord and put their trust in him and in Moses his servant." (Exodus 14:31)

Can you imagine this scene? A massive body of water 1600 feet deep literally split to create a huge opening with a dry path for thousands of people to walk through. But there's more! Once God's people were securely across the Red Sea, Moses raised his arms again, and the massive body of water returned, drowning the entire Egyptian army.

As we learned in our very first week, Moses was a reluctant prophet. But we can see, as his story unfolds, how God used him in mighty ways to save the Israelites, freeing them from Egyptian bondage. God's miraculous power moved the sea to save his people and also destroy the enemy, and he will go to any means to rescue you, too.

QUESTION

Have you seen or experienced a miraculous rescue? How did it affect your faith? Have you shared it with others?

PRAYER

Lord, we know you are the God of miracles, and we see your power through this story of the Israelites' deliverance. Thank you for all you do to rescue us from bondage. Amen.

DIG DEEPER

God Delivers the Israelites Out of Egypt — Exodus 12–14

Week 10 – Day Three

When he (the king) came near the den, he called to Daniel in an anguished voice, "Daniel, servant of the living God, has your God, whom you serve continually, been able to rescue you from the lions?" Daniel answered, "May the king live forever! My God sent his angel, and he shut the mouths of the lions."

— DANIEL 6:20–22A

Despite being captive in a cave of predators, God's faithful servant remained unharmed. God protected Daniel and, in the process, showcased his power for all to witness.

Daniel's courage and unwavering belief brought a whole nation to God as King Darius proclaimed, "I issue a decree that in every part of my kingdom people must fear and reverence the God of Daniel. 'For he is the living God and he endures forever; his kingdom will not be destroyed, his dominion will never end. He rescues and he saves; he performs signs and wonders in the heavens and on the earth. He has rescued Daniel from the power of the lions.'" (Daniel 6:26–27)

It's an incredible story and one you've likely heard in Sunday school. How is it possible that a man could be in the midst of lions and survive when others did not, as we see later when Daniel's accusers were thrown in? "And before they reached the floor of the den, the lions overpowered them and crushed all their bones." (Daniel 6:24b) The only explanation is God. He came to Daniel's rescue.

Because of Daniel's great faith, he found favor with the Lord and was shielded from any physical harm. God protects his people with a purpose, and this time it was to bring a whole nation to faith.

God is there to rescue and protect us, too. We just need to believe in the God of Daniel.

QUESTION

When has your trust and faith in the Lord resulted in his protection?

PRAYER

Lord, we know, as believers, that you protect us wherever we go and whatever we do. Thank you for your covering and, at times, for your dramatic rescue. Amen.

DIG DEEPER

Daniel and the Lions' Den — Daniel 6

Week 10 – Day Four

*About midnight Paul and Silas were praying and singing
hymns to God, and the other prisoners were listening to them.
Suddenly there was such a violent earthquake that the founda-
tions of the prison were shaken. At once all the prison doors flew
open, and everyone's chains came loose.*

— ACTS 16:25–26

They were praising the Lord in prison. It's not exactly where you
would picture a worship session, but Paul and Silas didn't care. Their
circumstances were secondary to their love of the Lord. And, because
of their great faith, God caused an earthquake to shake off their
shackles to free them.

You would think they would immediately run out of the prison
doors, but that's not what they did with their newfound freedom.
Instead, knowing that their jailer would be blamed for their escape
and likely killed, Paul and Silas remained in their cell and took the
opportunity to witness to all around them. In return, the jailer cared

for their wounds, and his whole family was baptized. In the morning, Paul and Silas were released. What a night in prison!

God rescued these faithful disciples, and he did it with a purpose—to bring others to him. Not only were the jailer and his household baptized, but many other prisoners were witnesses to all that had happened. Even the officials realized that something divinely ordained was going on and personally escorted Paul and Silas from the prison.

God will rescue you from your chains too—whether it be addictions, bad habits, worldly idols, relationships, etc. We just need to follow Paul and Silas' example to praise the Lord even when circumstances dictate otherwise.

QUESTION

What has caused you to be in bondage? God is in the business of freeing his people, so pray for his deliverance today.

PRAYER

Lord, thank you for breaking our chains that bind us to worldly ways. Empower us to use our deliverance to bring others to you, as Paul and Silas did. Amen.

DIG DEEPER

Paul and Silas in Prison — Acts 16:16–40

Week 10 – Day Five

The teachers of the law and the Pharisees brought in a woman caught in adultery. They made her stand before the group and said to Jesus, "Teacher, this woman was caught in the act of adultery. In the Law Moses commanded us to stone such women. Now what do you say?" They were using this question as a trap, in order to have a basis for accusing him.

But Jesus bent down and started to write on the ground with his finger. When they kept on questioning him, he straightened up and said to them, "Let any one of you who is without sin be the first to throw a stone at her."

— JOHN 8:3–7

They grasped their stones tightly and were ready to release. As her life hung in the balance, the religious leaders attempted to trap Jesus, making him choose between the Law and the life of a broken woman. But their plan backfired.

While being questioned, Jesus took a moment to pause and bend down to scribble on the ground. While we don't know what he wrote, we know that when he stood up, his response not only rescued the woman but reminded us all of a powerful truth. "For all have sinned and fall short of the glory of God." (Romans 3:23)

We, like this woman, need to be rescued from the death of sin. While the Pharisees were pointing their fingers toward the adulterous woman, Jesus redirected the focus back to them. With one statement, "Let any one of you who is without sin be the first to throw a stone at her," Jesus not only diffused the situation but set the woman free, as each accuser slowly dropped his stones and left.

Jesus is on a rescue mission to set captives free, just like he did with a disgraced woman who was about to be stoned.

QUESTION

Jesus' final words to the woman were, "Go now and leave your life of sin." (John 8:11b) Is there a sin that you need to leave behind?

PRAYER

Lord, thank you for loving us enough to reveal our sins and for reminding us of your ultimate rescue mission—the cross. Amen.

DIG DEEPER

Jesus and the Adulterous Woman — John 8:1–11

Take a Step

Rescue. Jesus rescued Peter while he was sinking fast into the stormy sea. An even more epic rescue occurred when God parted the Red Sea for Moses and the Israelites to escape their bondage in Egypt. Then, of course, there's Daniel and the Lions' Den, where God closed the mouths of lions to save his steadfast servant. God even caused an earthquake to break the prison gates and chains of Paul and Silas. And, with one statement, Jesus saved an adulterous woman from a certain death by stoning.

OUR LORD IS IN THE BUSINESS OF RESCUING HIS PEOPLE—AND HE DOES IT IN MANY WAYS. THE CROSS IS THE ULTIMATE RESCUE OF ALL AND OUR LASTING REMINDER. WHAT DO YOU NEED A RESCUE FROM TODAY?

STEP—WHAT SMALL STEP CAN YOU TAKE TODAY?

TRUST—WILL YOU TRUST AND SURRENDER TO THE LORD?

ENCOURAGE—WHO CAN ENCOURAGE YOU ALONG YOUR JOURNEY?

PRAY—PRAY FOR THE LORD TO GIVE YOU STRENGTH AND DIRECT YOUR NEXT STEPS.

Presence

And when they climbed into the boat, the wind died down.

— MATTHEW 14:32

Week 11 – Day One

And when they climbed into the boat, the wind died down.

— MATTHEW 14:32

The raging storm suddenly stopped. It must have been a dramatic moment as Jesus and Peter climbed into the boat. Immediately, Jesus' presence brought peace and calm. No longer were they being tossed about nor in need of a rescue. All was well around them, above them, and especially beside them.

When Jesus shows up, things change. Throughout the Bible we read about miraculous healings, dead bodies raised to life, and dramatic signs and wonders through tornadoes, storms, and lightning. Even a woman who had been bleeding for 12 years found healing as she touched Jesus' robe. Being in Jesus' presence not only can bring physical healing but spiritual healing as well. And, the good news is, we have access to his presence as we spend time in his Word and prayer.

To be in the Lord's presence is a gift that is available 24/7 to all who believe. In fact, God lives within us through his Holy Spirit, where peace abides—"The peace of God, which transcends all understanding ..." (Philippians 4:7a)

Even though storms may be raging around us, we can experience God's peace, anchored in his presence.

QUESTION

When in your life have you felt God's presence most strongly?

PRAYER

Lord, thank you for making your presence known when we need you the most. Help us to make meditating on your Word and prayer a priority so that we may feel your presence every day. Amen.

DIG DEEPER

Woman Who Touched Jesus' Robe — Matthew 9:18–26, Mark 5:25–34, Luke 8:43–48

Week 11 – Day Two

Even though I walk through the darkest valley, I will fear no evil, for you are with me; your rod and your staff, they comfort me.

— PSALM 23:4

You've heard these words—likely at a funeral. It's the beloved Psalm 23 written by King David, whose life started as a humble shepherd. David knew hard times, and his Psalms often reflect them. But this one has a hope-filled theme with a reminder that we never walk alone, "Surely your goodness and love will follow me all the days of my life, and I will dwell in the house of the Lord forever." (Psalm 23:6)

Whether we are trudging through a valley or celebrating on a mountaintop, God is with us. Many Scriptures remind us that he will never leave us nor forsake us. In fact, Jesus' final words of the Great Commission as he ascended to heaven were, "And surely I am with you always, to the very end of the age." (Matthew 28:20b)

God will never leave our side, but we don't always feel his presence. The many voices around us can drown out his divine whisper, and cultural noise can keep us busy and distracted. In fact, busyness has become a way of life for many, but God calls us to slow down—to take time to be in his presence.

Through Scriptures like Psalm 23, we can find comfort through our darkest valley days. His presence is a promise that we can lean into anytime. God is with us in the valleys and on the mountaintops—and right now.

QUESTION

Do you feel God's presence more in the valleys or on the mountaintops?

PRAYER

Lord, thank you for always being with us, whether we are struggling or celebrating. Slow us down so that we may hear your voice and feel your presence with us. Amen.

DIG DEEPER

Psalm 23

Week 11 – Day Three

"My ears had heard of you but now my eyes have seen you.
Therefore I despise myself and repent in dust and ashes."

— JOB 42:5-6

Job lost everything—his livestock, health, and even his children. It all happened one day without warning. As Scripture tells us, Job was "blameless and upright; he feared God and shunned evil." (Job 1:1) He had seven sons and seven daughters and thousands of animals— and lots of servants too. He was known in the land of Uz as a blessed and prosperous man. But that all changed when God allowed Satan to strip Job of everything.

You might be surprised by Job's initial response as he tore his clothes in mourning, "Naked I came from my mother's womb, and naked I will depart. The Lord gave and the Lord has taken away; may the name of the Lord be praised." (Job 1:21) Job was praising the Lord in his greatest time of loss. At least for a while.

Next, we see Job struggle as his wife and friends taunt him to discover what sin he must have committed to bring on this calamity. Although Job never curses God, he curses the day he was born and cries out, "I have no peace, no quietness; I have no rest, but only turmoil." (Job 3:26)

After 38 chapters of suffering and questioning, something happens that immediately changes Job's perspective. "Then the Lord spoke to Job out of the storm." (Job 38:1) And Job's response? "My ears had heard of you but now my eyes have seen you. Therefore I despise myself and repent in dust and ashes." (Job 42:5-6)

When Job had a personal encounter with the living God, no more questions were needed.

QUESTION

Have you had an encounter with God when you could undeniably feel his presence? What was your response?

PRAYER

Lord, sometimes doubt creeps in when we have our Job moments. Help us to see you in those trials to deepen our faith and trust in you. Amen.

DIG DEEPER

Job Loses Everything — Job 1 & 2
The Lord Speaks to Job — Job 38–41
Job Repents — Job 42

Week 11 – Day Four

Some men came, bringing to him a paralyzed man, carried by four of them. Since they could not get him to Jesus because of the crowd, they made an opening in the roof above Jesus by digging through it and then lowered the mat the man was lying on.

— MARK 2:3-4

They wrecked the roof for their friend. The room was filled beyond capacity, and they were desperate to get him to Jesus with no ground path possible. So they lifted their paralyzed friend onto a mat through the jam-packed crowd and up to the roof. Then, the destruction began.

When I first read this story, I had lots of questions: Did debris fall on anyone's head below? How did they even lower the paralytic on the mat down safely? Did they later fix or pay the bill to patch the roof? Of course, none of this is really relevant. The most important lesson is that these dedicated men knew the urgency in getting their disabled friend to Jesus, and they were willing to break down any necessary barriers to accomplish their mission. The unnamed friends believed that Jesus was the only one who could heal their paralyzed companion, and nothing was going to stop them. They knew the Lord's presence was all that was needed.

Thankfully, we don't need to wreck any roofs to get to Jesus, but sometimes there are other barriers, especially for those who don't yet believe. We, like the friends of the paralyzed man, are called to bring others to Jesus, removing any obstacles along the way.

QUESTION

Would you be willing to "wreck the roof" to bring someone to Jesus? What are the biggest barriers you face in bringing others to Christ?

PRAYER

Lord, we are thankful for these dedicated men who did what was necessary to get their paralyzed friend to Jesus. Empower us to be a "wreck the roof" friend to others. Amen.

DIG DEEPER

Paralyzed Man Lowered through Roof — Mark 2:1-12, Luke 5:17-26

Week 11 – Day Five

So the other disciples told him, "We have seen the Lord!" But he said to them, "Unless I see the nail marks in his hands and put my finger where the nails were, and put my hand into his side, I will not believe."

— JOHN 20:25

They called him Doubting Thomas for a reason. He needed proof. This disciple would not believe until he saw the visible scars on Jesus' hands with his own eyes. Those nail marks provided the evidence that Thomas needed to confirm that it was indeed Jesus.

A week after appearing to the disciples, Jesus did indeed show up to win over this doubter. When Jesus walked through a locked door, his first words to Thomas and the disciples were, "Peace be with you!" (John 20:26b)

When Jesus showed up, peace arrived with him. Jesus' presence and peace are impossible to separate. When we are in his presence, just like the disciples were, we are infused with his peace—and doubt disappears. Just ask Thomas who responded, "My Lord and my God!" (John 20:28)

While in this world, we may never stand face to face with Jesus like Thomas did, but his presence lives inside of us through the Holy Spirit. That is where we find our peace—and it all begins with belief.

Thomas refused to believe his fellow disciples and needed to see Jesus himself to be convinced. "Then Jesus told him, 'Because you have seen me, you have believed; blessed are those who have not seen and yet have believed.'" (John 20:29)

QUESTION

Do you continue to believe when God is silent and his presence seems absent? What has been your greatest time of doubt? How did you overcome it?

PRAYER

Lord, please help us to believe in you even when we don't feel your presence. We know you are always with us, and you bring peace through your Spirit. Amen.

DIG DEEPER

Jesus Appears to Doubting Thomas — John 20:24–29

Take a Step

Presence. When God shows up, there's an immediate impact. The moment Jesus entered the boat with the disciples, the raging storm ceased. Job instantly repented and fell to the ground in dust and ashes in God's presence. When Jesus met a group of dedicated men who wrecked the roof for their paralyzed friend, he performed a miraculous healing. And then there was Thomas, who doubted that Jesus had been resurrected until they came face to face with each other.

BEING IN THE LORD'S PRESENCE CHANGES SITUATIONS— AND LIVES. ARE THERE BARRIERS THAT YOU NEED TO REMOVE TO GROW IN YOUR RELATIONSHIP WITH JESUS? HOW CAN YOU HELP REMOVE BARRIERS FOR OTHER PEOPLE TO MEET THE LORD?

STEP—WHAT SMALL STEP CAN YOU TAKE TODAY?

TRUST—WILL YOU TRUST AND SURRENDER TO THE LORD?

ENCOURAGE—WHO CAN ENCOURAGE YOU ALONG YOUR JOURNEY?

PRAY—PRAY FOR THE LORD TO GIVE YOU STRENGTH AND DIRECT YOUR NEXT STEPS.

Worship

Then those who were in the boat worshiped him, saying, "Truly you are the Son of God."

— MATTHEW 14:33

Week 12 – Day One

Then those who were in the boat worshiped him, saying, "Truly you are the Son of God."

— MATTHEW 14:33

All they could do was worship. Jesus showcased his power over creation, calming the winds and the seas. The disciples had seen miracles before, but this one was dramatic, immediate, and impacted their lives directly. As they worshiped him, they reaffirmed his divine identity, "Truly you *are* the Son of God."

Worship. As humans, we are made to worship. But our affections can easily become misdirected. We worship created things, not the creator of it all. The object of our worship may become our spouses, children, celebrities, politicians, or even our jobs.

In recent years, it has become a cultural norm to worship the "universe." But in this miraculous story above, the disciples got it right. They knew who controlled the wind and the seas and the only one worthy of worship—the Son of God.

God desires us to worship only him. In fact, he made it clear in his Ten Commandments. The very first commandment states, "You shall have no other gods before me." (Deuteronomy 5:7) This serves as a necessary warning: What we worship can eventually become our own personal god, as our identity gets attached to that idol instead of the Lord.

The second commandment says that we are not to deify anything created, "You shall not bow down to them or worship them; for I, the Lord your God, am a jealous God, punishing the children for the sin of the parents to the third and fourth generation of those who hate me, but showing love to a thousand generations of those who love me and keep my commandments." (Deuteronomy 5:9–10)

God takes worship very seriously and, as believers, we should too. He alone desires our worship.

QUESTION

What worldly gods are you tempted to worship? How can you refocus on the one true God?

PRAYER

Lord, there are many idols in our world that can take our focus away from you. Help us to anchor our identity in you and focus our worship on you alone. Amen.

Week 12 – Day Two

Wearing a linen ephod, David was dancing before the Lord with all his might, while he and all Israel were bringing up the ark of the Lord with shouts and the sound of trumpets.

— 2 SAMUEL 6:14–15

He danced in the streets! David didn't care who was watching. He was single-mindedly focused on praising and worshiping his Lord. He had stripped himself of his royal garments—wearing a priestly linen ephod instead—as he led the holy ark carrying the Ten Commandments into Jerusalem. David's focus was solely on pleasing the Lord.

But someone was not happy. David's wife Michal, daughter of Saul, watched from above, "And when she saw King David leaping and dancing before the Lord, she despised him in her heart." (2 Samuel 6:16b) He was not acting nor looking like a proper king and, as his wife, she was not pleased and let him know it immediately upon his return home.

But despite his wife's disapproval, David responded to Michal, "It was before the Lord, who chose me rather than your father or anyone from his house when he appointed me ruler over the Lord's people Israel—I will celebrate before the Lord." (2 Samuel 6:21) It was a mic-drop moment. David knew his first allegiance was to the Lord, and he wasn't going to be led astray—even by his wife.

Despite David's failures as a father and other epic mistakes (see the story of Bathsheba in chapter #9), he repented and lived his life to please the Lord. God called David a man after his own heart (1 Samuel 13:14), and we clearly see why through this story.

King David worshiped to an "Audience of One."

QUESTION

When you worship, are you single-mindedly focused on the Lord or more concerned about what others around you may think?

PRAYER

Lord, thank you for this example of David, who unabashedly loved and worshiped you. Strengthen us to be steadfast in our worship, no matter who is watching. Amen.

DIG DEEPER

The Ark Brought to Jerusalem — 2 Samuel 6

Week 12 – Day Three

Then Miriam the prophet, Aaron's sister, took a timbrel in her hand, and all the women followed her, with timbrels and dancing. Miriam sang to them: "Sing to the Lord, for he is highly exalted. Both horse and driver he has hurled into the sea."

— EXODUS 15:20–21

They were singing praises to the Lord. God had just rescued the Israelites from Egypt in a dramatic scene, parting the Red Sea. Now it was time to celebrate! As Moses and the crowd broke out in song, Miriam, the first prophetess mentioned in the Bible, takes it a step further and adds an instrument and dancing. For all practical purposes, Miriam had become the first worship leader!

You may not have heard of Miriam, but she played a key role in freeing the Israelites. As Aaron and Moses' older sister, she watched over her baby brother Moses as he floated down the Nile River in a basket where Pharaoh's daughter found him. (Exodus 2:4) Next

Miriam arranged for her mother to be Moses' nursemaid, so they could remain close and protect him within the palace walls. (Exodus 2:7) That is the last time we hear about Miriam for the next 80 years, until she reappears for the Red Sea celebration.

Although Miriam's daily influence is not mentioned in Scripture, we know she had a big impact and was a recognized leader—in a time when woman were considered inferior to men and without equal rights. But God raised her up: "I brought you up out of Egypt and redeemed you from the land of slavery. I sent Moses to lead you, also Aaron and Miriam." (Micah 6:4)

QUESTION

When you think of a celebration, do you think of worship? When your Red Sea moments arrive, do you stop to give glory to God?

PRAYER

Lord, help us to remember you in our times of celebration. We know that every good and perfect gift is sent from you, so remind us to always give you the glory. Amen.

DIG DEEPER

Red Sea Celebration — Exodus 15:1–21

Week 12 – Day Four

"My soul glorifies the Lord and my spirit rejoices in God my Savior, for he has been mindful of the humble state of his servant. From now on all generations will call me blessed, for the Mighty One has done great things for me—holy is his name."

— LUKE 1:46–49

It is known as "Mary's Magnificat," meaning "my soul magnifies the Lord" in Latin. It is a hymn of praise found in Luke 1:46-55 and can be heard in Catholic, Lutheran, and Anglican services, as well as read in the Book of Common Prayer used in many Christian churches. In it, Mary glorifies the Lord and speaks of his mercy, power, and promises. She calls herself blessed, but the story didn't start that way.

When the angel Gabriel first appeared to Mary, she was "greatly troubled." (Luke 1:29) In fact, the angel told her not to be afraid as he explained how she would give birth to a son who would rule over

David's kingdom. Mary's fear then shifted to confusion, "'How will this be,' Mary asked the angel, 'since I am a virgin?'" (Luke 1:34)

Once the angel had departed her, Mary took a road trip to see her cousin Elizabeth who was already with child—John the Baptist. And it was in Elizabeth's presence that Mary shared her beautiful tribute to the Lord.

Sometimes what God calls us to do causes fear, especially when we don't understand. But even through her fear and confusion, Mary responded with obedience and then later followed with worship. And we get a glimpse of her strong faith as her song is saturated in Scripture. No wonder she was highly favored!

QUESTION

Has God's calling ever caused you fear or confusion? Like Mary, was worship a part of your response?

PRAYER

Lord, we thank you for Mary's response to worship you even when she was afraid and confused. Help us to trust and praise you no matter what. Amen.

DIG DEEPER

Angel Appears to Mary and Mary's Song of Praise — Luke 1:26-56

Week 12 – Day Five

Therefore, I urge you, brothers and sisters, in view of God's mercy, to offer your bodies as a living sacrifice, holy and pleasing to God—this is your true and proper worship.

— ROMANS 12:1

Worship. It's not just something we do on Sundays. It involves sacrificing our lives to please God—*every day*. Just ask the apostle Paul who embodied this kind of "living sacrifice" as he encountered great suffering and obstacles while taking the gospel message all the way to Rome. He was beaten, imprisoned, attacked, and faced opposition every step of the way. Paul knew that true and proper worship, pleasing to God, would not be easy. It required complete devotion, reverence, adoration, suffering, and submission to God's will.

As Paul reminds us, worship is not just singing, attending church, and lifting our hands in praise—although these are acts of worship. Worship is our response to what God is doing in our lives. In fact everything we do can be considered an act of worship: "So whether

you eat or drink or whatever you do, do it all for the glory of God."
(1 Corinthians 10:31) True worship is a lifestyle focused on pleasing
the Lord.

So how do we make worship a lifestyle, reflected in our daily lives?
According to Paul, it involves sacrificing our bodies—our talents, our
possessions, our jobs, our physical attributes, our personalities, everything that is a part of us—to God's plan, not our own.

True worship is surrendering our wants to God's will, praising him,
and making sacrifices every step of the way.

QUESTION

What does worship mean to you? How are you living it out?

PRAYER

*Lord, thank you for Paul's example of true and proper worship. Let us
strive to live our lives as a sacrifice to you—to praise and glorify you in
all that we do. Amen.*

DIG DEEPER

Paul on Sacrifice, Service, and Love — Romans 12
Paul on Living a Christlike Life — Colossians 3

Take a Step

Worship. It was their only response when Jesus calmed the storms and seas. It was also what David couldn't help but do when he danced his way into Jerusalem with the Ark of the Covenant. Miriam and Mary worshiped through song, praising the Lord for his rescue and favor. But Paul, most of all, understood that true worship is a sacrifice of your whole being. It is a lifestyle.

HOW DOES YOUR LIFE REFLECT A LIFE OF WORSHIP TO OUR LORD AND SAVIOR?

STEP—WHAT SMALL STEP CAN YOU TAKE TODAY?

TRUST—WILL YOU TRUST AND SURRENDER TO THE LORD?

ENCOURAGE—WHO CAN ENCOURAGE YOU ALONG YOUR JOURNEY?

PRAY—PRAY FOR THE LORD TO GIVE YOU STRENGTH AND DIRECT YOUR NEXT STEPS.

Invite a Friend

For where two or three gather in my name, there am I with them.

— MATTHEW 18:20

Introduction

Despite a storm swirling around them, Peter was in the safest available option at the time—the boat. Without Jesus' invitation, Peter would have stayed put. But with one word, "Come," Jesus invited him out of his comfort zone to grow in his trust—with a step out onto the daunting waves.

So, why not extend an invitation, like Jesus did, for a friend to join you on this journey to walk on water? Discussion often brings new perspectives and opportunities for growth, so I am providing a space here for just that.

While this book was written as a personal devotional, the following pages contain questions to discuss with a friend to grow deeper in your relationship with the Lord.

It's time to walk on water—together.

Week 1

Immediately Jesus made the disciples get into the boat and go on ahead of him to the other side, while he dismissed the crowd.

— MATTHEW 14:22

Our theme this week is "Send," and our lessons provided many examples of Jesus sending people out into his world. Jesus sends us into circumstances, to individuals, and sometimes even into storms. But he always sends us with a purpose—"To make disciples." (Matthew 28:19) Where is Jesus sending you right now?

WHICH DAY'S LESSON SPOKE TO YOU THE MOST? WHY?

REVIEW THE RECAP TOGETHER AND SHARE YOUR STEP WITH EACH OTHER.

HOW CAN YOU ENCOURAGE AND PRAY FOR EACH OTHER THIS WEEK?

Week 2

After he had dismissed them, he went up on a mountainside by himself to pray.

— MATTHEW 14:23A

Our theme this week is "Pray," and our lessons provided not only a model for prayer but many examples of the importance of prayer. How is your prayer life? What are your obstacles to making prayer a daily priority?

WHICH DAY'S LESSON SPOKE TO YOU THE MOST? WHY?

REVIEW THE RECAP TOGETHER AND SHARE YOUR STEP WITH EACH OTHER.

HOW CAN YOU ENCOURAGE AND PRAY FOR EACH OTHER THIS WEEK?

Week 3

Later that night, he was there alone, and the boat was already a considerable distance from land, buffeted by the waves because the wind was against it.

— *MATTHEW 14:23B–24*

Our theme this week is "Storms," and our lessons provided many examples of how biblical characters endured the storms in their lives —some better than others. Do you grow bitter or better through them? What will you do differently in the future to grow closer to the Lord through the trials that will inevitably come?

WHICH DAY'S LESSON SPOKE TO YOU THE MOST? WHY?

REVIEW THE RECAP TOGETHER AND SHARE YOUR STEP WITH EACH OTHER.

HOW CAN YOU ENCOURAGE AND PRAY FOR EACH OTHER THIS WEEK?

Week 4

Shortly before dawn Jesus went out to them, walking on the lake.

— MATTHEW 14:25

Our theme this week is "Seek," and our lessons provided many reminders of how Jesus is always seeking us, despite our disobedience at times. Are you as eager to pursue the Lord? What are you actively doing to grow in your relationship with the Lord?

WHICH DAY'S LESSON SPOKE TO YOU THE MOST? WHY?

REVIEW THE RECAP TOGETHER AND SHARE YOUR STEP
WITH EACH OTHER.

HOW CAN YOU ENCOURAGE AND PRAY FOR EACH OTHER
THIS WEEK?

Week 5

When the disciples saw him walking on the lake, they were terrified.

"It's a ghost," they said, and cried out in fear.

— MATTHEW 14:26

Our theme this week is "Fear," and our lessons provided many examples of fear-filled people in the Bible. Fear is a normal physiological response, but being paralyzed by fear or allowing it to drive your decisions is not. How do you respond to fear? What take-away do you have from this week's lessons that can help you when fear creeps in?

WHICH DAY'S LESSON SPOKE TO YOU THE MOST? WHY?

REVIEW THE RECAP TOGETHER AND SHARE YOUR STEP WITH EACH OTHER.

HOW CAN YOU ENCOURAGE AND PRAY FOR EACH OTHER THIS WEEK?

Week 6

But Jesus immediately said to them: "Take courage! It is I. Don't be afraid."

"Lord, if it's you," Peter replied, "tell me to come to you on the water."

— MATTHEW 14:27-28

Our theme this week is "Courage," and our lessons provided many examples of common people who God positioned and then empowered for his purposes. How has God positioned you right now to further his kingdom? Are you leaning on his strength or your own?

WHICH DAY'S LESSON SPOKE TO YOU THE MOST? WHY?

REVIEW THE RECAP TOGETHER AND SHARE YOUR STEP WITH EACH OTHER.

HOW CAN YOU ENCOURAGE AND PRAY FOR EACH OTHER THIS WEEK?

Week 7

"Come," he said.

— *MATTHEW* 14:29A

Our theme this week is "Invite," and our lessons provided many examples of Jesus' appeal to all who crossed his path, including children. With his words, "Follow Me," he was then—and is today— inviting all who are interested to a life-changing transformation. How has your life changed as a result of following Jesus?

WHICH DAY'S LESSON SPOKE TO YOU THE MOST? WHY?

REVIEW THE RECAP TOGETHER AND SHARE YOUR STEP WITH EACH OTHER.

HOW CAN YOU ENCOURAGE AND PRAY FOR EACH OTHER THIS WEEK?

Week 8

Then Peter got down out of the boat, walked on the water and came toward Jesus.

— MATTHEW 14:29B

Our theme this week is "Obey," and our lessons provided many examples of biblical characters who responded with obedience when the Lord called them to action. God is calling you too and has created you with a purpose and a plan. Obeying God's calling is a daily decision. What is your natural reaction when you know God is calling you into a specific situation or to a specific task?

WHICH DAY'S LESSON SPOKE TO YOU THE MOST? WHY?

REVIEW THE RECAP TOGETHER AND SHARE YOUR STEP WITH EACH OTHER.

HOW CAN YOU ENCOURAGE AND PRAY FOR EACH OTHER THIS WEEK?

Week 9

But when he saw the wind, he was afraid and, beginning to sink, cried out, "Lord, save me!"

— MATTHEW 14:30,

Our theme this week is "Focus," and our lessons provided examples of those who were steadfastly focused on the Lord and his purposes as well as others who were distracted with their circumstances and surroundings. What are practical ways that help you keep your focus on Jesus and his eternal purposes and not worldly distractions? To help you "be in this world but not of this world?"

WHICH DAY'S LESSON SPOKE TO YOU THE MOST? WHY?

REVIEW THE RECAP TOGETHER AND SHARE YOUR STEP WITH EACH OTHER.

HOW CAN YOU ENCOURAGE AND PRAY FOR EACH OTHER THIS WEEK?

Week 10

Immediately Jesus reached out his hand and caught him. "You of little faith," he said, "why did you doubt?"

— MATTHEW 14:31

Our theme this week is "Rescue," and our lessons provided many examples of how Jesus rescued and protected his people. With our sinful nature and godless influences around us, we need God's protection, and—at times—his rescue. How does knowing that God protects you affect your daily life? How do these stories encourage you to grow deeper in your relationship with Jesus?

WHICH DAY'S LESSON SPOKE TO YOU THE MOST? WHY?

REVIEW THE RECAP TOGETHER AND SHARE YOUR STEP
WITH EACH OTHER.

HOW CAN YOU ENCOURAGE AND PRAY FOR EACH OTHER
THIS WEEK?

Week 11

And when they climbed into the boat, the wind died down.

— MATTHEW 14:32

Our theme this week is "Presence," and our lessons provided many examples of how God's presence changed circumstances—and lives. Even if we don't feel his presence, he is with us. How does knowing that God walks with you every day change your life? Priorities? Career? Relationships?

WHICH DAY'S LESSON SPOKE TO YOU THE MOST? WHY?

REVIEW THE RECAP TOGETHER AND SHARE YOUR STEP
WITH EACH OTHER.

HOW CAN YOU ENCOURAGE AND PRAY FOR EACH OTHER
THIS WEEK?

Week 12

Then those who were in the boat worshiped him, saying, "Truly you are the Son of God."

— MATTHEW 14:33

Our theme this week is "Worship," and our lessons provided many examples of people worshiping the Lord. Worship is not only something we do at church on Sundays, it's a lifestyle. How does your life embody one that worships the Lord? If it doesn't, what do you need to change?

WHICH DAY'S LESSON SPOKE TO YOU THE MOST? WHY?

REVIEW THE RECAP TOGETHER AND SHARE YOUR STEP WITH EACH OTHER.

HOW CAN YOU ENCOURAGE AND PRAY FOR EACH OTHER THIS WEEK?

About the Author

Julie Osborne is an inspirational Christian author and passionate Bible study teacher. Her deep love for God's Word forms the anchor of her writing ministry. With her debut devotional, *Walk on Water: A 12-Week Devotional on Trust, Turbulence, and Fixing Your Eyes on Jesus*, she aims to inspire and empower readers to navigate life's turbulence by trusting the Lord completely.

Her writing career began as an editor, feature writer, and special projects manager for *Current Publishing* in Carmel, Indiana, where she published hundreds of articles. Her unique voice, blending inspiring faith with humorous personal essays, has been celebrated in publications like *Chicken Soup for the Soul, Guideposts' Angels on Earth Magazine, Pet Pals TV*, and the *Erma Bombeck Humor Writers* blog.

Julie has always felt a special connection to stories of faith and adventure, evident in her blog, *Tales of Oz*. A year after the blog's launch a real-life divine encounter occurred: a rescue dog named Toto arrived on her lap. Coincidence? She thinks not! Now, "Oz and Toto" are working together to share their story in their debut children's book, *Toto Finds Home*.

Oz and Toto invite you to follow their adventures through their website and social media channels and be on the lookout for more books. They are just getting started!

Connect with Me

Julie and her beloved dog, Toto.

Website: https://www.julieosborne.com

instagram.com/ozandtoto
facebook.com/authorjulieosborne
youtube.com/@authorjulieosborne
linkedin.com/in/author-julie-osborne

www.ingramcontent.com/pod-product-compliance
Lightning Source LLC
Chambersburg PA
CBHW060419130626
46555CB00005B/2125